Everywhere You Go People Are the Same

by Jacob G. Orfali

RONIN
Berkeley, Ca.

Everywhere You Go. People Are The Same
Copyright 1993 by Jacob G. Orfali
ISBN Pbook: 9780914171751
ISBN Ebook: 9781579512804

Published by:
RONIN Publishing, Inc.
PO Box 3436
Oakland CA 94609

Project Editor:	Sebastian Orfali
Editors:	Judy Abrahms & Ginger Ashworth
Cover Design	Sebastian Orfali
Layout:	Ginger Ashworth
Cover Art:	Generic Typography

Dedication

To my children who treasure the privileges provided in these United States of America (God's Own Country).

Appreciation

A special appreciation is due to my son Sebastian whose valuable efforts made the realization of this book possible.

Jacob G. Orfali, the author, at age 50.

Introduction

I was born in Jerusalem, of Armenian parents who survived the first genocide of this century, that of the Armenian people at the hands of the Turks. The story of my family and early life appears in my book *An Armenian from Jerusalem*.

I am married to Stephanie, who fled Nazi Germany in the early 1930s and escaped the holocaust that engulfed many among her friends and family. Her story is recounted in her book *A Jewish Girl in the Weimar Republic*. We have four children, and came to the U.S.A. in 1957, after knocking around the world. We moved to Napa in 1979 to flee the cold winters of Northern Illinois, where we lived for twenty years, and also to be near two of our sons who live in Berkeley.

This book contains the story of my travels and the lessons I learned from people all over the world.

Wherever you go, the aim of the people is basically the same. They want to be able to afford the necessities required for the well being of their loved ones. It is the exploitation by a few, who take advantage of the tolerance of the majority, that destroys the harmony. Nature provides enough resources for every living being to enjoy a contented life. Modern law courts dispense legal opinions instead of justice. Treatment of employees by their employers is usually influenced by legalism, not fairness.

The world forgets that in death, humans depart with an open palm of the hand. You cannot take it with you. So, be generous to your loved ones and kind to your fellow man.

Table of Contents

Sisters Rita (left) and Justine (right) in Bethlehem

Everywhere You Go, People Are the Same

Chapter 1.
Sister Rita

Looking back down memory lane, I have a vivid and fond recollection of our dear friend Sister Rita. She was born in northern Italy. She did not resemble Italians from her looks. She was tall, blond, and had clear blue eyes and a permanent smile. A nun in the French order of St. Joseph, she was assigned to their convent of Bethlehem, not far from the church of Nativity of Jesus. My aunt Justine was also a nun in the same convent and they were very good friends.

I first met Sister Rita when I was a young boy, visiting my aunt Justine with my mother and her sisters. She came into the reception room, carrying a serving tray with glasses of liquor for the grownups and a glass of lemonade for me; there were also pieces of fruit sweetmeats on the tray. When she offered, I picked up the glass of lemonade and a piece of sweetmeat from the tray. Sister Rita urged me to pick up a piece of each kind of fruit.

While the other sisters were transferred to other convents, Sister Rita and my aunt stayed in Bethlehem all the time.

After Steffi and I got married, I visited my aunt Justine in Bethlehem, accompanied by my wife. Into the reception room came Sister Rita who offered us wine and cookies she had made. I complimented her on the delicious wine and cookies. As we left Sister Rita presented us with a bag containing a bottle of her wine and cookies to take home.

At the time of hostilities in Jerusalem due to the Partition Resolution, we left our house that was on the borderline of the two hostile parties and took refuge in the St. Joseph convent in Bethlehem.

During our stay in the convent we got to know the many talents of Sister Rita. She was the provider of the goodies. Before making wine, she would make several trips to the vineyards, to test the sugar content and acidity of the grapes. They were harvested only when she was satisfied that they were ready to be crushed for wine. She made the most palatable liquors with herbs and fruits grown in the convent's garden, as well as different types of cookies, sweetmeats, hams, and sausages. She was also the music and art teacher. Her pupils performed well-attended musicals, appreciated by their parents and guests. They also created inspired paintings on canvas and silk.

During our stay in Bethlehem, she would often ask me to go with her to the cellar, to sample her newly made wine. We would start sampling her latest raw wine and progress to the past years to compare. We emerged from the cellar with a much happier disposition than when we went in.

It seems that she had a special touch; her wines have always succeeded. The Salisians (Italian fathers of John Bosco), besides running a trade school, had a commercial winery. When it came to making wine for mass, they often asked for Sister Rita's assistance.

We left the holy land in 1951. We went back for a visit in 1970. We enquired about Sister Rita from my aunt Justine. We were told that she was transferred to Ramleh, a town on the way to Tel Aviv. She was happy to receive us with her proverbial smile. She told us she was teaching music to the Israeli young girls, immigrants from North Africa. They flocked in from the surrounding towns to study music.

God bless you, dear Sister Rita, wherever you are. Thank you for bringing sunshine into the life of people who had the privilege of knowing you.

Arthur Braun, the father of Stephanie Orfali

Chapter 2.

Arthur Braun

Arthur Braun was born in Niederstäten, South Germany, in 1883, the ninth of ten children. He attended four years of elementary and three years of high school education. His father had a liquor store and café combined. He also dealt in animal skins and furs, which Arthur collected from the farmers in a one-horse cart that he drove around. He hated the chore, because he had to carry cash with him for paying the farmers, and was always afraid of being robbed.

Arthur later joined his older brothers in Nuernberg in their furniture factory. He picked up the trade very quickly and he was later accepted as an equal partner.

As was the custom he met and married Martha Bernhard through a match-maker. Unlike other girls, who had never met their future husbands, Martha had dancing lessons with Arthur in the same dancing school.

A few years after getting married, Arthur separated from his brothers, by opening his own factory. He had a successful business when the Nazis came to power and confiscated everything. He started a travel agency and helped many Jews to leave Germany to all parts of the world. He was well known at the British consulate, which had issued visas to enter Palestine to many of his customers. They readily issued him and his wife an immigration visa to Palestine, waiving all the required formalities, when he had to leave Germany shortly before the outbreak of WWII. My wife Steffi and her brothers Wolfgang and Heinz were already in Palestine, and the youngest son Werner was in Denmark.

Arthur did not like it when I, a non-Jewish Armenian, married his only daughter. He reconciled with it later. One would wonder, "What is an Armenian doing in Jerusalem?" The answer is, the Armenians were the first, as a nation, to accept the Christian faith. Thereby they had acquired very strong ties to the Holy Land. As Christians, they were the only nation in the Middle East who were allies of the Crusaders. The two first Christian queens of the Crusader kingdoms of Jerusalem were Armenians. The Armenian king Hetoun II of Cilicia occupied the Holy Land with his troops for the period of 1300–1303 after defeating the Sultan Housameddin of Egypt. On Mount Zion the Armenian Monastery of St. James covers an area of 300 acres, or one-fifth of the space of the old city of Jerusalem. A large number of Armenians took refuge in the monastery of St. James after WWI when fleeing the Turkish genocide of the Armenians. (For more details about the Armenians, please refer to *An Armenian from Jerusalem* by the author.)

During the first year of our marriage, Steffi and I lived with her parents. Arthur spoke only German, Martha spoke some English and French, but we communicated in German. Arthur first opened a travel agency but had to give it up due to the outbreak of WWII. He then started a soap and cosmetic business. He had salespersons call on homes to get orders that were brought to my mother-in-law, Martha, who filled them in a spare room in the apartment where we lived that was converted into a store room. The orders were delivered the next day. Steffi took care of the shopping and preparing the meals.

Arthur was an absent-minded person, especially during meals— his mind was somewhere else. When he wanted cheese, bread, salt, or something else that was on the table, he would just point to it. At the end of the meal, he would ask his wife, "Mama bin Ich satt?" which means Mother am I satisfied or satiated? He reminded me of the professor, who entered the toilet with a book in his hand; when he came out, he had the toilet seat under his arm. Arthur always carried a small notebook and a tiny end of a pencil in his breast pocket. He often stopped what he was doing, took out the notebook, and scribbled something in it. It brought to my mind the story of the professor who sat outside the delivery room, while his wife was giving birth. He hears the cries of a baby, the nurse appears, saying, "Congratulations Professor, your wife just gave birth to a baby boy." The professor jumps to rush to his wife. The nurse stops him with these words: "There is more coming." The professor sits down and consults his notebook, he hears a second baby's cry, followed by the appearance of the nurse, who says, "Professor, your wife gave birth to a second healthy boy." The professor answers with a grunt, and keeps his nose in the notebook. The nurse, losing patience, asks him, "Don't you want to be with your wife?" Without lifting his eyes from the notebook the professor answers, "Not yet, there is more coming."

Due to some trouble with his throat, Arthur was exempted from military service during WWI. He made good money by converting his furniture factory into making wooden shoes for the German army. When he saw the crowded streets of Jerusalem full of allied soldiers, he got a brain storm. That evening he asked me to help him write a letter in English to the military distribution center, offering his services as supply contractor to the armed forces. He received a reply within a few days informing him that his offer was being considered. They gave an identification number for him to use in dealing with them in the future. After a while orders started coming. A letter came from the military distribution center asking for bids for the supply of goods listed on an attached sheet. He received his first order based on the bids that he sent in. He received regular orders thereafter. This made him a de *facto* supplier to the armed forces.

Arthur could not make a living with the money he earned from the supplies to the military. He needed a telephone for his other deals, but it was almost impossible to get a new line during the war. I suggested that I try to apply for a phone for him, giving his military-supply business as a reason for preferential treatment, and it worked. While other applicants waited for a phone for many months, Arthur Braun got his phone within a week. It was a big step forward for the business.

During the whole years of the war things were very quiet in the Holy Land. Toward the end of the war, the situation began getting ugly. The Jews insisted that Palestine be open for all their brethren, victims of Nazi persecution, which the Palestine British administration resisted. There ensued confrontation between the British and Jewish nationalists, resulting in the United Nations resolution to partition Palestine into two states (Arab and Jewish). The Jews accepted and the Arabs rejected the Resolution. The armed conflict was now between Jews and Arabs. The Jews that lived in Arab quarters moved to the Jewish section of Jerusalem and the Arabs moved from the Jewish to the Arab section.

At this time Arthur and Martha who lived in a Jewish quarter had to pass through some Arab quarters to commute from home and back. They and their neighbors were evacuated with British protection into the Jewish section. They needed a home badly. Arthur had heard of an empty house in the Jewish section whose Arab-Christian owner had just moved out to the Arab section of Katamon. He asked me to help him rent it. It so happened that the owner's son used to work in the same company where I had. I asked him to arrange for an appointment for us with his father. Arthur and myself travelled by bus full of unsuspecting Arabs, rented the house from the owner, Mr. Barnich, who offered us brandy to seal the deal. Much later we realized that it was unwise of Arthur as a Jew to go with me to Katamon in view of the precarious situation of the land.

The house stayed in the family Braun until it was demolished by a developer, who had to compensate Arthur for the loss of his dwelling and also to let him have an apartment in the new building at a much-reduced price. The apartment was sold after my mother-in-law Martha passed away and the proceeds were divided between her grandchildren.

In the early 1950s, the Germans returned the properties confiscated from the Jews by the Nazis, and compensated them for loss of income. Arthur travelled to Germany and hired a lawyer, who got him the highest settlement for his factory, etc., allowed by German law. Opa (as grandfathers are called in German) was suddenly extremely rich. While traveling by train he got to conversing with an old man who was in his cabin. It happened that this person was coming from East Germany where the communists took away his very well-known Wella hair dye and cosmetic factory. He intended to build a new factory in Damstadt, West Germany, and was looking for some investors. Opa made a deal with his new acquaintance, whereby he was given a license to produce and sell all Wella products in Israel and also to be the sole representative of the company in the neighboring countries. The production factory was built in Israel for making Wella products per company specification mixed from raw materials sent from Germany by technicians trained in the main factory. It is proudly shown to visitors as a model Israeli industry by Teddy Kolek, mayor of Jerusalem. It is now administered by Heinz Braun, second son of Arthur, and his children.

Opa was a very generous person. He loved his family, but he was brought up in a culture where men insisted that their wives be virgins at betrothal, whereas they indulged in all kinds of sexual activities before marriage and continued seeing other women thereafter.

He always said that he would strive to see that his wife would be well provided for before passing away, and by God, he succeeded.

Jerusalem Christian Brothers College during 1949–1950.

Everywhere You Go, People Are the Same

Chapter 3.

Moving to Bethlehem

I mentioned in my book, *An Armenian from Jerusalem*, that we lived in a British military zone after the outbreak of the hostilities as a result of the partition resolution of Palestine by the United Nations. Next to our house was the sergeants' mess of the British Military Police. We did them favors; civilian areas were out of bounds for them for security reasons. My wife Steffi would shop for them; she would buy women's wear such as silk nightgowns, nylon stockings, and other lingerie for their loved ones—items unobtainable back home in England on account of the rationing. They would buy for us from the NAAFI, "similar to U.S. military PX," items not obtainable in the market. In other words, we had good neighborly relations.

One night in April, 1948, I heard some scratching noises on our front door, as if somebody wanted to come in. He was either too shy or unwilling to knock, wanting to avoid making noise. I opened the door; the second in command of the Military Police was standing outside. He asked in a whisper permission to come in. Once in, he closed the door behind him and said, "Jacob, this will take only a couple of minutes. Two weeks ago, on a hunch, you warned me not to accompany the night patrol. As you know, the patrol vehicles struck a land mine. I came to tell you that we received orders to vacate our quarters in two weeks' time. I urge you to move before that time. If you don't your family will be hurt."

I replied, "I appreciate your warning. I know that once you leave, we will no more have protection of the military zone, both belligerent sides (Arabs and Jews) would try to occupy this area. We definitely don't want to be in the middle of the fighting, but where do you suggest that we go?"

He said, "I have a hunch that Bethlehem is of no strategic value to any of the parties. I know you have an aunt who is a nun in a convent there; I am sure she will be able to help you get a refuge until things return to normal."

I thanked him profusely and gave him a hand-carved scene of the Last Supper and crosses all made from mother-of-pearl, a specialty of Bethlehem work. I always kept a stock of such souvenirs handy, to give as presents. He was speechless. He told me he wanted very much to buy such souvenirs from the Holy Land to take home, but did not have access to them. We hugged, wishing each other good luck, and he disappeared quietly in the darkness and I went to bed.

Having obtained permission from the Mother Superior of the St. Joseph's Convent, I took my family to Bethlehem to avoid exposure to the dangers that were brewing. I went back to my mother's house in the old city of Jerusalem. My brothers had relocated their business to Amman, Jordan, from Jerusalem; my mother and youngest sister joined them. I was the only occupant of the whole big house.

I spent an unforgettable fortnight in the old city; the nights were shattered by explosions all around the house from falling mortars. Luckily, houses in Jerusalem are built with solid rock and are not easily damaged. I could not sleep at all the first night; eventually, I got used to the noise and it quit bothering me. It reminds me of the German proverb, "Der Mensch is ein gewohnheits tier," man is a creature of habit.

The Socony-Vacuum Oil Company, where I worked, paid us two months' wages on May 13, 1948. We were told that the company was suspending its operations temporarily and that we would be recalled as soon as things returned to normal. Instead of staying in the old city, I took a bus to Bethlehem the next day, May 14, to join my family.

I was now faced with the problem of finding a place to sleep. I

Everywhere You Go, People Are the Same

could not stay in the convent, it being cloistered and out of bounds to men at night. I could spend the day somehow, but sleeping quarters for the nights were at a premium, for Bethlehem was flooded with refugees like us. The Mother Superior had an inspiration. She asked me if I had a gun. "Yes," I answered, "I left it in my mother's house in Jerusalem; civilians are severely punished when found carrying guns." She said, "My plan depends on your having a gun."

I went back to Jerusalem and picked up my gun (a Smith and Wesson revolver). When I got to the area to take transportation to Bethlehem, it was deserted. A few minutes before two P.M., a private car with two young men pulled up. They appeared to be looking for somebody. I asked the driver if I could ride with them to Bethlehem, and he replied that he would be glad to take me if I would wait until his friend arrived who was due to be there any minute. We saw his friend coming toward the car; he jumped in the back seat where I was already installed, and we took off.

In order to take the Bethlehem highway, we had to cross a kind of "no-man's land" between Talpioth, a Jewish settlement protected by armed guards, facing their Arab opponents from the side we would emerge, and the highway. The Arab guards stopped us; they asked if we were carrying any weapons. We said no, and just as they were ordering us to get out of the car to search us, the Jews started shooting from Talpioth. The Arab guards took cover, shouting, "Move on, don't stop!" Our driver sped through a hail of bullets—luckily, they were not aimed at us.

In Bethlehem, the Mother Superior received me with a big smile and said, "You are now our second night guard. You will be sleeping in one of the classrooms outside the cloister. The Bishop agreed to this arrangement."

The convent had a paid night guard who was an ex-French legionnaire. Michel came every night at seven and patrolled the grounds surrounding the buildings. He left at seven the next morning.

People were unemployed; many were forced to resort to illegal means to earn a living for their families. All the other convents in

Bethlehem were broken into and we felt that our turn would come. After all, we were only two males in the convent, whereas the convents of the Christian Brothers, the Salesian Fathers, etc., who were all males and were supposedly better able to protect their property, were all robbed. I usually spent a few hours with the guards at night after my family retired; then I went to the classroom and lay on a cot reading, and went to sleep after midnight. We could hear shooting and cannon shots exploding all around Bethlehem at night, but things were quiet in the city itself. I remembered very often my British Military Police friend and his hunch. I wondered loudly to myself: "What a hunch!"

Bethlehem was supplied with electric power from Jerusalem: the generating station fell into the hands of the newly formed Israeli forces on the night of May 15, 1948, and they cut off all the supply lines outside their jurisdiction. Other than candles, kerosene lamps were the main source of light. One night I had just extinguished my kerosene lamp and was beginning to doze when I heard Michel shouting outside the window, "Monsieur Jacques, monsieur Jacques, please come, bring your gun!"

I put on my morning gown, took my gun and ran with bare feet to meet him. He said, "Thieves, two of them!" and ran. I followed him. They had vanished by the time we reached the place he had seen them. They had left behind a canvas bag containing some pots and pans which they had stolen from the kitchen. They had been spotted by one of the girls, who heard noises from an open window on the second floor while on her way to the bathroom. She looked out of the window and saw two men, one of them carrying a canvas bag. That is when Michel heard her shouting, "Thieves, thieves!"

It later transpired that Michel had passed the same spot a few minutes before. They must have seen him and taken cover. We looked all over the convent grounds, then climbed to the top of the poultry yard and looked down the street. I saw two black forms stuck to the wall below us. I put my index finger on my mouth to alert Michel not to speak, and pointed out the two forms to him. I whispered to him that we should just scare them off without harming them. I shot two bullets into the air; they moved closer to the wall. We could see them shaking and we felt as if the wall under us was shaking too.

Then we began a charade. I asked Michel loudly, "Do you have a sharp knife, Michel?" He said, "Yes, monsieur Jacques—why?" I answered, "We will emasculate them as soon as we catch them, and then we will string them on that big oak tree. We will hand them over to the Jordanian authorities in the morning, you know how harsh the Jordanians are." (At that time, Bethlehem was occupied by the Jordanian army.)

We pitied the two would-be thieves, who kept shaking. By this time we had recognized them as soft-spoken, harmless neighbors, forced to steal to provide food for their families. After a while I said, "Michel, it seems we will not be able to find them, they must be far away by now. Let's get out of here!" We could hear their long breaths of relief as we left.

After that night, no attempt was made to rob the St. Joseph Sisters' Convent. Warning must have been spread to would-be thieves that the convent was guarded by two fierce and heartless guards.

Damascus reception for Socony Vacuum (Mobil Oil)

Chapter 4.

Beirut

I was born of Armenian parents in 1915, in the Holy City of Jerusalem, while it was under Turkish Ottoman rule. On December 11, 1917, the Allied forces under General Allenby entered Jerusalem after defeating the Turks. In the year 1923, it became the capital of the British Mandate of Palestine. The name Palestine derives from that of the Philistines, pre-Hellenic Greeks, who inhabited the area in Biblical times. The Old Testament recounts the romance between Samson, the Israelite judge, and Delilah, a Philistine woman. For the first few years of British rule, peace and harmony prevailed, as promised by General Allenby. My life in this period is told in the book *An Armenian from Jerusalem*.

The world Jewry insisted that the British fulfill the promise of their Balfour Declaration, which was the creation of a Jewish homeland in Palestine. Naturally, the natives resented this plan. Harmonious neighborly life was soon replaced by distrust and conflict. The situation got out of hand when the British issued a new Palestinian currency to replace the currency introduced at the time of occupation. The new currency bore English, Arabic, and Hebrew inscriptions. The Hebrew inscriptions had the equivalent of E. and I., meaning Eretz Israel (land of Israel). An English Jew, Herbert Samuel, was appointed High Commission of Palestine, to represent the British Crown. Centuries-old mixed neighborhoods were destroyed and segregated enclaves created. The British, who had made conflicting promises to both sides, did not seriously attempt to negotiate a peaceful settlement. Perpetual unrest in the country would justify continuation of British occupation of the country. At that time, the British did not wish to let go of their mandate, it being a vital artery link to India.

Finally, in 1947, the United Nations passed a resolution that partitioned Palestine, dividing it between the native Palestinians and the newly created State of Israel. This division was to take place on May 15, 1948. The British moved out on the eve of May 15, leaving chaos behind them.

At this time I was working for the Socony-Vacuum Oil Company (Mobil Oil) in Jerusalem. The company gave us notice, with two month's advance pay, shortly before May 15. We were told that we would be called back once the situation had stabilized. Bombing and firefights had begun between the Palestinians and the Israelis soon after the Partition Resolution of 1947. The Palestinians rejected the partition. They announced that they would fight to keep all of Palestine.

My family lived on the borderline between the two warring factions, in Jerusalem. We decided to move to Bethlehem for a while, hoping to return when things returned to normal. We still have the house key we took with us, but we never returned to use it.

Bethlehem is a very small town, supported largely by the tourist trade. It was full of Jerusalemites like us, and there was no way for us to earn a living. Our savings dwindled. Finally I was offered a position at the Christian Brothers' College in Jerusalem, teaching business administration and foreign languages—and monitoring the boarders' dorms at night—for the school year of 1949–1950. I considered myself fortunate and accepted readily, though the job would separate me from my family, whom I could see only on weekends in Bethlehem.

In June of 1950 I was asked by Socony-Vacuum to return to work for them, this time in Beirut, Lebanon. Shortly after my arrival, I was transferred to Damascus, Syria. My family remained in Bethlehem, which at this time was occupied by the Jordanians.

In the spring of 1951 the Syrians refused to renew my work permit, and as a foreigner I was no longer allowed to work in

Damascus. I went back to Beirut and got a better-paying job, this time at United Nations headquarters, where my varied work experience was appreciated. My family joined me in Beirut, happy to return to modern living after two years of primitive existence and privation in Bethlehem.

Departure from Beirut

In the summer of 1951, Riad El Solh, the former Muslim Prime Minister of Lebanon, was assassinated in Amman, Jordan. Muslims became incensed and attacked the Christian quarter in Beirut, looting and burning private homes. A week later, King Abdullah of Jordan was killed in the Temple Place in Jerusalem, where he had gone for his weekly Friday prayers in the Mosque of El Aksa. This time the Lebanese Army surrounded the Christian quarter and prevented the Muslim demonstrators from getting out of hand. These assassinations remain a mystery.

My late father had lived through similar upheavals. Remembering his cautionary advice, I resolved to leave the Middle East before it erupted in a bloodbath. This did in fact occur later on and Lebanon has been engulfed in Civil War for over a decade. At the time, my wife and children were outraged by my decision. They hated to give up the good life they were living in the metropolis: swimming in the Mediterranean, hiking in the mountains, weekend outings, easy transportation, abundant gourmet food. My mind was made up, though. The future welfare of our family demanded that we sacrifice our pleasant life and my good job.

At the time, Brazil was the only country that would issue us an immigration visa without delay. We applied for one and received it at once. My boss at the United Nations was disappointed when I told him of my decision to leave. He tried to sway me by promising me a future job in Lake Success, the U.N. headquarters in New York State, but I declined his offer. When he realized I wouldn't change my mind, he said, "Jacob, you still have your refugee status." This status had been granted me when I left my home in Jerusalem to flee the conflict resulting from the partition of Palestine. "That means," he explained, "that you and your family qualify for free passage, which will be paid by the Special Immigration Fund of the United Nations." He told me whom to see to make the arrangements, and my application was quickly approved.

My mother and brother Leon had moved from Jerusalem to Amman, Jordan, with the rest of the family. They came to Beirut from Amman to share our last days with us and see us off.

Before we left, I met an Armenian friend in Beirut. He had just returned from São Paulo, Brazil, which was our destination, so he had a great deal of vital information to pass on to a new immigrant. Most important, he told me I would be able to get a job easily through the American Chamber of Commerce, even though I could not speak Portuguese, the language of the country.

On the day of our departure, an employee of the United Nations met us at the harbor to give us our boarding passes for the S.S. Corinthia—a Greek ship—and $350 pocket money. We were assigned a comfortable second-class family cabin that easily accommodated the six of us: myself, my wife Stephanie, eleven-year-old George Michael, nine-year-old Gabrielle Marie, five-year-old Joseph Sebastian, and our ten-month-old baby, John Paul.

The ship lifted anchor and sailed westward into a golden sunset, as the crowd of well-wishers shouted their farewells and waved their handkerchiefs. The passengers called back to them, and we were on our way.

We explored the ship with the children, who were very excited by this adventure. Then we tucked them into their beds and went to the bar for a drink. We were exhausted, and soon went to bed ourselves.

Jacob Orfali and family with Joseph Orfali and a lady passenger, posing before Notre Dame De La Guarde in Marseilles during 1951

Jacob Orfali

Everywhere You Go, People Are the Same

Chapter 5.

The Mediterranean

Alexandria

Alexandria was a sleepy fishing village when Alexander the Great landed there during his conquest of Egypt in the Fourth Century B.C. He was impressed by the naturally protected harbor and ordered the construction of a fortified town on the shore. General Ptolemy was left behind to supervise the task while Alexander pushed forward into Egypt. After Alexander's death, Ptolemy continued to rule the area on behalf of Alexander's son, Alexander Aegos. Upon the death of Alexander Aegos, Ptolemy seized power and became the ruler of Egypt. Under Ptolemy Soter, Alexandria began its rise to fame as a great city of culture and learning. The great Museum and Library of Alexandria were founded and the city became an important Mediterranean seaport. It is still a major port today. St. Mark, the patron saint of Alexandria who preached Christianity to Egypt, is buried in Alexandria. A manuscript believed to be the original Gospel of St. Mark is kept in the Coptic Cathedral of the city. The Copts are descended from the early Christians. Their name is derived from the name "Aegypt," given to them by the Greeks.

Alexandria was ruled by the Ptolemies until the reign of Cleopatra VII, celebrated in literature for the beauty that captured the heart of Julius Caesar and Marc Antony. She committed suicide in 31 B.C. rather than surrender to the Roman emperor Octavian, whose victory ended Greek rule of Alexandria.

We arrived in Alexandria at dawn. The Egyptian authorities

issued passes to the passengers for visiting and shopping in the city. We rented a horse-drawn carriage; little Gabrielle had a toothache, so our first stop was the office of an Armenian dentist recommended by the ship's steward. After that we went to the zoo, a treat for the children, who had never seen a real zoo before. We lunched in an Egyptian restaurant, drove around on the boulevards, and returned to the ship fully content.

Our next stop was Port Tewfic, on the Suez Canal, where we basked in the sun on the ship's deck while its fuel tanks were filled for the journey ahead.

The ship crossed the Mediterranean Sea for three days, passing several islands. During this time we got acquainted with our fellow passengers, played cards, lay in the sun, and enjoyed a life of leisure.

Greece

We docked at Piraeus on the fourth day. Piraeus is the port city of Athens, five miles southwest of the Greek capital. Themistocles persuaded the Athenians to fortify Piraeus and use it for their fleet in 403 B.C. Axis troops occupied the port in April 1941. It was bombed heavily during World War II. We took the tram to Athens, the political, economic, and cultural center of Greece. Together with Piraeus, Athens is the center of rail, road, and sea transport. Athens was named for the city's patron goddess, Athena, goddess of wisdom.

In Athens we visited the Acropolis. In the Greek language Acropolis means "the city at the top." It is comprised of fortifications and temples. Destroyed by the Persian invaders, these were rebuilt after the victory of Eurymedon in 468 B.C. A collection of archaic statuary, vases, and the beautiful little temple of Athena Nike was added to the original. The temple of Athena was demolished by the Turks in 1684 and its stones built into a Bastion. In 1835 the temple was reconstructed faultily by L. Ross on the removal of the Bastion. It was dismantled and rebuilt accurately between 1935 and 1940.

We picked up some pieces of marble from the ruins for souvenirs. We still have them. We had lunch in a picturesque Greek restaurant, where we were served lamb shishkebab and a mixed salad of tomatoes, cucumbers, goat cheese, and olives. We drank ouzo, the Greek "firewater." We then watched the changing of the guards in their colorful uniforms.

At sunrise the next morning the ship left Piraeus, sailing past sleepy Ionian islands. We could see the smoke rising from the villagers' huts, where they were starting fires for breakfast. Soon we came to the Corinthian ship canal, where a tugboat towed the ship through the narrow passage between steep cliffs. This canal was opened in 1893 to provide sea communication between Corinth and Patras, the Ionian islands and Athens. As we passed under a bridge, we were greeted by children who tossed candy down to the ship. We enjoyed the scenery, the relaxed atmosphere, and the mild weather.

The next morning we were in the Mediterranean. The ship must have encountered a rough sea as it came into open water, because the deck lights, signaling an alert, were still on when we awakened. We docked in Genoa, Italy, before noon.

Genoa

Genoa (Genova), capital of the province of Genoa and chief port of Italy, is situated on the Gulf of Genoa. It has a long history of different occupants. Destroyed by the Carthaginians in 209 B.C., it was restored by the Romans, who made it the headquarters of their fleet.

The Genoese were famous seafarers. They established colonies as far away as the Caspian Sea. Among Genoa's famous sons were Andrea Dorio, Christopher Columbus, and Nicolo Paganini. Letters from Columbus and a violin that belonged to Paganini are exhibited in the Palazzo Municipale, built by Rocco Lurago at the end of the 16th Century.

We left the ship and took a streetcar to the old city. There we saw the house where Columbus was born. We went window-shopping in the old city and ended up at a *condittoria*, where we splurged on exquisite Italian cookies, cappucinos, and Cassata ice cream. When we returned to the ship, our friends asked us whether we had visited the cemetery to see the beautiful sculptures on the family mausoleums. We admitted we hadn't. They told us we'd missed a once-in-a-lifetime chance to appreciate great art.

Marseilles

The next day the ship reached Marseilles, its final destination on this voyage. Marseilles is the chief seaport of southern France, on the Mediterranean. It was settled by the Phoenicians. It derives its name from the Greek colony of Massilia, founded in 600 B.C. by the mariners of Phocaea in Asia Minor. It was Christianized by the end of the Third Century. Ravaged by a series of invaders, it finally came under the protection of its viscounts in the Tenth Century, paving the way to a stable native administration.

Occupied by the Germans in November 1942, Marseilles was liberated by the Free French in August 1944. When American soldiers returned home from the war in 1946, more than a million of them embarked from the port of Marseilles.

A pleasant surprise awaited us when we landed: my brother Joseph was there to welcome us. We had written to him from Beirut, telling him our departure date and the name of the ship, but we were dumbfounded when we actually heard him call my name and saw him run to us, open-armed, welcoming us in Armenian. Joseph had left Jerusalem in 1933 to study medicine in Paris. He never returned to the Holy Land. First there was the unsettled situation in the country. Then the invading Germans imprisoned him as an alien, the holder of a British Palestine passport. He was interned with other British subjects in St. Denis, near Paris. After the war he had married a Frenchwoman and received French citizenship. He lived in Sèvres, a short distance from Paris.

After the first shock ended, I introduced Joseph to my family. There was much kissing and hugging. They were very happy to meet him in person at last, having heard so much about him.

Joseph told us he had taken a room in the hotel we were to stay in. He had learned of our destination from the travel agent at the Messageries Maritimes, which was in charge of our trip to Brazil. Let me mention that all our children were fluent in the French language, which they learned when we lived in the French convent in Bethlehem. They could easily follow our conversation with their newly discovered Uncle Joseph.

At the hotel we had a pleasant time reminiscing and exchanging the latest family news. Joseph told us he and his family were living with his father-in-law, who was a widower and a retired French government employee. This kindly man had insisted that Joseph come to Marseilles to meet us.

The next day we had our first chance to visit a public bathhouse. These are used in all the great cities of Europe by people who do not have bathtubs at home. We had had no facilities for bathing on the ship, and the hotel provided by the travel agency had no bathtubs either. Our accumulated dirty clothes were washed after we returned to the hotel. In the afternoon, Joseph took us to La Canebière, the hub of the city. We had some refreshments at a department store, where we bought some things for the transatlantic voyage and a portable baby carriage for our youngest son. As we walked back to the hotel, we saw an amusement park and took the children in. They were thrilled: they had never been to such a place in their lives.

The side streets between La Canebière and our hotel were inhabited by North Africans. These streets were dangerous at night, and we were counseled to avoid them. Several times we passed a castle built by Napoleon III for the Empress Eugénie. We saw some unforgettable views of the harbor and the city.

On our second day in Marseilles we visited the Ancienne Cathédrale de la Major, with its impressive ceramic ornaments, the 15th Century altar of Lazarus, and the tomb of Bishop Xavier of Belsance, who diligently assisted the victims of the plague that struck Marseilles during the 18th Century. We then took the cog-elevated railway to the Basilique de Notre Dame de la Garde, which crowns the Gulf of Lions, and beside it a fortified projection into the bay that protected the harbor. The steeple of the Notre Dame de la Garde church is topped by a 30-foot gilded statue of the Virgin. It rises 150 feet above the summit of the hill.

We also took a motorboat from Quai des Belges to Chateau d'If, celebrated by Alexandre Dumas in his novel, The Count of Monte Cristo. Here we saw the Count's prison cell and that of the Abbé d'Arles, who was also a prisoner, and with whom he communicated.

Our stay in Marseilles was very enjoyable and we were in high spirits when we resumed our voyage to Brazil, aboard the S.S. Florida, a large French ship, which had carried troops during World War II and had recently been commissioned to carry civilian passengers. This ship was fully booked by refugees from many areas, including Germany, Italy, Palestine, Syria, Lebanon, and the countries of Eastern Europe.

Upon boarding the ship our family was separated. My wife and children were placed in a cabin that had been designed to hold 10 passengers, but was occupied by 14 people. I shared a cabin with an old Lebanese man who was returning to Brazil after a visit to his native country.

The S.S. Florida was a very comfortable ship, manned by an experienced crew. It belonged to the Messageries Maritimes French government-owned company. Very little entertainment was offered, and it had a very small bistro or bar where drinks and cigarettes could be bought. In short, it was a strictly immigration ship.

We witnessed a disturbing incident on our first meal on the S.S. Florida. The meals were served in a large refectory, in two groups at different sessions, assigned to the passengers. The waiters started serving as soon as all were seated, beginning with the table near the entrance. Some noisy young men were seated at this table, they emptied the whole bread basket next to their dishes, filled their glasses with the wine served with French meals, did not pass the carafe to their neighbors, they kept the soup tureens as well. Without comments, the waiters brought more bread, wine, and soup to the rest of this table. At this point, the embarrassed rowdies shut up completely and we began savouring our meal. This incident was never repeated; on the contrary, there was a complete change of attitude in these so-called thugs. They sometimes went out of their way to please their neighbors. They were especially kind to the women and children.

We later heard that the ship steward had called their leader to his office, and gave him a serious talk, saying, "There is plenty of food and drinks for everybody on a French ship; they could always ask the waiters for a second serving (not that this is a necessity—the waiters will do it automatically). The inconvenience of the other passengers will not be tolerated."

Barcelona

Barcelona is the capital of Catalunia, a province on the eastern Mediterranean coast of Spain. Most traffic to and from Europe from Spain moves through Barcelona. The Moors captured Barcelona in 713 and it was reconquered by the Franks in 803. Eventually it became one of the foremost trading cities on the Mediterranean, rivaling Genoa and Venice. Christopher Columbus' small fleet sailed out of Palos for the New World on August 3, 1492, and returned there, to an enthusiastic welcome, on March 15, 1493. Columbus marched in triumph from Seville to Barcelona, where at the end of April he was received in solemn splendor by the King and Queen of Spain.

Our ship reached Barcelona before noon. We left the harbor to visit the cathedral at the center of the old city. We passed through the Puerta de la Paz, next to the 199-foot Columbus Monument, erected for the International Exhibition of 1888. This monument overlooks the port. We saw solemn religious processions in the streets, and were reminded that it was the last Sunday in October, dedicated to the Missions by the Catholic Church.

After the cathedral, we took a quick trip to explore the ambitious project of the architect Antonio Gaudi, the Templo Expiatori de la Sagrada Familia (Church of the Holy Family), whose shapes were inspired by those of plants and animals. This edifice was begun in 1882 and has not yet been completed. If it is ever finished, it will look like a model we saw in the crypt. We would have liked to visit the world-famous Museu Picasso, where the artist's progress can be followed from his early sketchbooks to the poster for his last exhibition. We would make that trip 35 years later, on our next visit to Barcelona, but now we had to return to the ship. Incidentally, the cab that carried us around Barcelona was fueled by natural gas from a large tank of carbon in the trunk.

We sailed out of Barcelona and passed through the Strait of Gibraltar late at night, under a full moon. We passed through what the ancient Greeks called the Pillars of Hercules. The Rock or Gib (as it is now known to the British) is one of the Pillars; the other is Jabal Musa (the Mountain of Moses), known as Apes' Hill in English. Twice as high as Gibraltar, Jabal Musa is located on the African coast near Ceuta. To the ancients, the Pillars were the boundary of the known world.

Gibraltar (Jabal Tariq in Arabic) is named after Tariq ibn Ziyad, a Muslim general who in 711 set sail with his soldiers and horses in four borrowed boats from Ceuta, on the African side. He set up a beachhead below the Rock, where the town of Gibraltar is located today, then ferried in the rest of his army, totaling 12,000 troops, and invaded Spain.

Overlooking Rio de Janeiro and the Sugar loaf mountain at the opening of Guanabara Bay

Orfali family in Tucuruvi, São Paolo, Brazil in 1956

Everywhere You Go, People Are the Same

Chapter 6.
The Atlantic

After crossing the strait of Gibraltar, we entered the vast expanse of the Atlantic Ocean. The S.S. Florida veered south, destination Dakar, capital of Senegal, which at that time was still a French colony. In the meantime, the passengers had lots of leisure. They got acquainted, made new friends, and exchanged rumors about neighbors in the same cabins and chose their preference of people to associate with for the duration of the trip, and got accustomed to the daily routine. The women were allowed into the laundry room for two hours a day to do their washing. My wife Steffi was advised by a new-found friend to tip the sailor in charge. When she did, he let her use the laundry room alone, at another time of the day, to do our family washing (especially our youngest son, John's, diapers). Our oldest son George who spoke fluent French, besides German, Arabic, and Hebrew, got himself a job as helper to the Pastry baker and supplied the family with all kinds of pastry destined for the ship's officers. He also translated into German and Arabic for the benefit of non-French speaking passengers the announcements made in the French language, on the public speaking system. We reached Dakar in a few days.

Dakar

Dakar (now the capital of the Republic of Senegal) is one of the chief seaports on the West African coast. It is also the ocean terminal of railroads. Its position midway between Europe and

South Africa and South America is appreciated by ships and planes. We took a walk to an open-air market passing by a sewer trench that polluted the atmosphere. I bought a large snakeskin already tanned, for investment, which a friend of ours later sold in Sweden. I also bought some mystical carvings on black wood. We were back in time before the ship left for Brazil.

Onward to Brazil

Up to that time, I had no steady companion other than my family. I avoided the Bistro, as I was not a drinker, and did not enjoy the noisy ambiance. My cabin partner was an old uninteresting ignorant man, who kept boasting about his boring business experiences in Brazil. To pass the time, I took long solitary walks on the deck of the ship, reliving past experiences in my life.

Once when walking around the ship, I came upon my son George who was conversing in German with a young man. He introduced himself as Father John, a newly ordained missionary priest on his way to Bahia in northern Brazil, where he was assigned to serve. I met Father John again the next day, while on my daily walk. During our conversation he informed me that he was born a Jew, was saved by a Catholic priest who smuggled him into a convent where he was brought up with other boys his age. He attended classes with the boys, some of whom may have been Jewish. He was warned not to speak about his background, just do like the others. Though he had to attend religious services, they did not pressure him to accept the Catholic faith, and when he expressed his wish to be baptized after a few years of living in the convent, they told him to reconsider it. He repeated his wish six months later, and was given the same reply as before. He got his wish after he expressed it for the third time. An entire year had elapsed since he had expressed his desire for baptism for the first time. A few years later he was accepted on probation in a seminary. After he proved his sincerity they let him study for the priesthood. He had been ordained a year ago. When he opted for missionary duty, he took a special training. He was now on his way to Brazil to fulfill his yearning. I asked Father John, being born Jewish, how it felt to be a Catholic priest. He said, "The same as the first disciples who were born Jews, or St. Paul who turned from the fiercest persecutor of the early Christians into the staunchest propagator of the Christian faith. St. Paul was the champion of the Universality of Christianity, instead of keeping it exclusive to those born Jewish, as some of the early church leaders of Jerusalem wanted to keep it. He said, 'The Messiah came to redeem the whole of mankind, not only the Jewish people.' He broke down the imaginary barrier and said, 'Welcome to the club' to everybody who joined. There are many prominent members in the Catholic church hierarchy who are of Jewish origin, such as the Cardinal Archbishop of Paris, France. There was even a pope of Jewish origin. In one word, I feel very comfortable."

On another occasion, I asked Father John what he thought about the Jews accusing Christians of worshiping idols such as the statues, and images of Jesus, Mary, and other saints.

Father John said, "Christians do not worship idols, they venerate Jesus, Mary and the saints represented by the statues and images. It is a psychological impulse, the same way as people keep pictures of dear ones both dead and alive. The Jews keep their scrolls in very ornate enclosures; is it because they worship the scroll or they venerate it because it is the Holy Book? Let me tell you that there were very exquisite mosaics in the floor of the early Jewish synagogues, before the Christian era. One of them was recently discovered in archaeological digs near Jericho in the West Bank of the Jordan."

I said, "What is your opinion of superstition? I read about Jews, who place their newly born son in a cot made out of reed or hay to influence their growing into a Moses or the Messiah. Actually, my French niece, on hearing that her Jewish boss's son sleeps in a cot made of hay, asked her father to call me from France, to enquire if I had heard of such a Jewish custom."

Father John replied, "Every nation has its own legends which may have started as rumors or gossip, and ended up as myth which people believe to be real. For instance, some Jews believe that their dead in the cemetery rise up at night to discuss the folks left behind. It is also said that at Yom Kippur (Day of Atonement) the departed even join the living in the synagogue and lament for their sins. People listening to these gossips are tempted to believe them, and some do. This reminds me of Tevye, the milkman in *Fiddler on the Roof.* When the wealthy widower butcher asked Tevye for his daughter's hand and they drank to it, it made his wife very proud. But his daughter was very unhappy and refused to go along. She wanted to marry the undernourished tailor who was as poor as a church mouse. Tevye promised his daughter that he would find a way out. During the night, he feigned having nightmares and started shouting, which woke up his wife. She inquired what was the matter. He told her that he was visited by her long-departed aunt who said that the butcher's dead wife is very much against their daughter marrying her husband and does not give her peace. Her departed aunt was tormenting him in his dream, insisting on cancelling the agreement. Thus Tevye succeeded in getting his wife's consent for going back on their promise to the butcher. Even though people knew the whole dream was a scam, they accepted it."

I often encountered Father John on my morning walks. We greeted each other and continued each one on our way. I stopped him once and said, "I would like to ask your opinion about Moses whom the Jews refer to as their teacher. The Hebrew saying 'Abraham abenu Moshé morénu' means Abraham our father, Moses our teacher. I read in the *Antiquities of the Jews* by Josephus Flavius that, as Egyptian field marshal, Moses made war against Ethiopia and won. He married Tharbis, the daughter of the King of the Ethiopians, who admired him. The Egyptians, jealous of his fame, conspired for his destruction. When Moses got wind of the Egyptian scheme, he fled out of Egypt into Midian. Sigmund Freud in his book *Moses and Monotheism,* suggests that Moses may not have been a Jew, but an Egyptian prince, who admired King Amenhotep IV. Amenhotep IV, who strived to introduce monotheism into Egypt, changed his name to Ikhnaton. Aton was the name of the one god to be worshipped. He instituted this practice among his followers. I have also read somewhere that after the Ethiopian campaign, Moses was rewarded with the post of governor in an area adjoining Midian. I also read that is how he knew of the monotheism practised by the tribe of Jethro their priest, whose oldest daughter Zippora he later married.

"Herodotus visited Egypt about 450 B.C. He writes about the strange customs of the Egyptians, among them circumcision. Moses as Egyptian was himself circumcised. He instituted this practice among his followers, the Jewish people he guided out of Egypt. What about the Covenant and circumcision of Abraham and descendants mentioned in Genesis 17–18? It is suggested that the Israelites who created the text of the Bible did not know the fact that circumcision originated in Egypt.

"Ernst Sellin, in his book *Mose und seine Bedeutung für die israelitich-judiche Religionsgeschichte* discovered in the book of the prophet Hosea unmistakable traces of a tradition that Moses was killed in a rebellion by his stubborn people. All these do not reconcile with the text we read in the Bible."

Father John said, "Christians must believe what is written in the Old Testament, and the coming of Christ our Savior is the fulfillment of the prophecies. Ours is the continuation of the old Jewish religion. Both Sigmund Freud and Ernst Sellin are Jewish authors. If you still are interested, I advise you to consult a Talmudist." (Talmudists are Jewish scholars who study all the commentaries about the Bible of old and modern sages. They dedicate their life to discuss the Torah or Old Testament with other Talmudists, and write new revised commentaries.)

"Let me tell you what Sigmund Freud said about Talmudists," I said. "Quote: Scholastics and Talmudists are satisfied to exercise their ingenuity, unconcerned how far removed their conclusions may be from the truth," I added.

"Okay. Father John, we both have had enough of this for one day. Let me buy you a drink at the Bistro," I concluded.

"I accept," said he. "That is the least you can do after all the grilling and hard time you gave me."

All this, of course, was said in a spirit of fun and friendship.

Crossing the Equator

At midday, our ship was scheduled to cross the equator, an imaginary line on the surface of the earth midway between the north and south poles. It is customary to have some festivities aboard ships crossing the equator, when passengers crossing for the first time may be initiated to become members of the International Society of the Sons or Daughters of the Equator. It is also an occasion to break the monotony, resulting from many days of the same horizon of an endless sea covered by the tiresome blue sky. It is amazing to watch the change of attitude of the passengers toward each other, as if their inborn prejudices never existed. They all worked side by side for the success of the coming festivities and had a good time doing it. The lack of a common language was overcome by signs used for communication, resulting in loud laughs and tapping on the backs. The whole action was under the supervision of the ship's steward, who must have been trained in psychology. On one side of the ship's deck, a group of Arabic-speaking youngsters, joined by some Europeans, were having a good time practicing the "Dabkeh" (a cadenced dance) to the tune of a flute made of reed. Next to this group, Greek passengers dressed as "evzones" (picturesque white jackets, wide skirts, and slippers with turned-up tufted toes) practiced a group dance shouting, "Aera! Aera!" Nearby a Portuguese group, each member in his turn, was practicing the "Fada" (songs of lament, which the Portuguese must have learned from their North African Muslim conquerors). These are some of the scenes crowding the ship's deck, looking like an active "beehive." At 12 noon a procession started consisting of an old member of the crew venerably dressed like the legendary Neptune, King of the Seas, with his trident scepter. He was preceded by a band of music, surrounded by an entourage of the ships' officers elegantly dressed for the occasion. Neptune acknowledged the applause of the crowd with his broad grandfatherly smile. The cortege proceeded to a large space on deck where Neptune mounted the throne (a golden armchair exquisitely decorated with sea life).

A group of Italians dressed like fishermen from Naples (Napoli) followed Neptune. There were four of them, two mandolin and one guitar players, and a solo singer. They came to the open space, which served as a stage, singing the Santa Lucia (the song of Naples). Next the soloist took over with songs praising the generosity of Father Neptune and thanked him for the inexhaustible bounty of sea food that Naples is blessed with. It saved the Neapolitans from starvation, when they were under the yoke of different foreign greedy occupiers of their land, besides the endless beds of corals that bring in badly needed dollars to sustain the present sick economy in the area. The finale was a very emotional reprise of Santa Lucia, which drove the watching public into wild frenzied applause.

Next came a Spanish group. They began with songs from the opera Carmen, a scene of a toreador fighting a bull, and finished up dancing the bolero accompanied by singers and guitar music. There was also a side comic show of some young men shaving a bridegroom before his wedding. They used a large pail containing leathery soap water, rubbed the bridegroom's face, eyes and head with foam of the soap with the aid of floor brushes, and feigned shaving him with a large open razor made out of wood. It was a hilarious scene. The jittery bridegroom on his chair was pinched all over his body, while his buddies made funny remarks. It was a successful and relaxing afternoon which brought out the best behavior of the passengers and contributed to making lasting friendship between people of different languages and cultures. It was amazing to observe how people who avoided fellow passengers out of fear or ignorance, became friendly and enjoyed the companionship of the same individuals. This is one thing air travelers miss nowadays. It confirms the existence of human brotherhood, when unhindered by special interests.

We began seeing small islands with vegetation in the ocean the next day and the day after we saw the first flights of birds to announce that we were nearing Rio de Janeiro.

Jacob (second from right) inspecting the work at a hydroelectric power plant in Cubatão, Brazil

Everywhere You Go, People Are the Same

Chapter 7.

Arriving in Brazil

Rio de Janeiro

Its full name is São Sebastião de Rio de Janeiro. Port city and capital of the republic of Brazil until 1960, when Brasilia became the new capital. Having a natural harbor, the city is in a plain between a group of mountains: the Serra da Carioca and the wooded heights of the Serra do Mar. Sugar Loaf mountain (Pão de Açúcar), at the entrance of the Bay rising 1,296 feet, is between the city and the Atlantic coast. On the highest point of the Carioca range which partly divides the city is Mount Corcovado (Hunchback) at 2,310 feet on whose summits towers the imposing statue (98.5 feet high) of Christ the Redeemer.

The entrance to the bay is between the Sugar Loaf and the Pico do Papgaio (Parrot's Beak). When the ship anchored in the harbor the health officers and relatives of some of the passengers came aboard, among them the parish priest of the Armenian Catholic community of Rio de Janeiro. I introduced myself to the Armenian Catholic priest. When he heard I was from Jerusalem, he informed me that Father Gabriel who baptized our son Joseph Sebastian in Jerusalem, was now parish priest in São Paulo, our destination.

Upon landing we took the streetcar to the foot of the Corcovado and boarded the cog-wheeled train to the top on the mountain. We visited the place of the Statue of the Redeemer, and enjoyed the awe-inspiring view of the surrounding panorama. We would have liked to visit the Sugar Loaf but had to go back to the ship after visiting the world-famous beaches of Copa Cabana.

Santos

We left Rio de Janeiro at dusk for Santos, where we would land and head for the city of São Paulo, our final destination. Santos is a seaport of the state of São Paulo. Its docks of four miles can accommodate a large number of steamers at one time. It is linked with the state capital city, São Paulo, by a very efficient railway system and a magnificent highway, the Via Anchieta. Its leading export is coffee, whose aroma permeates the city. Its annual tonnage of shipping exceeds that of Rio de Janeiro. Its warehouses can store 5 million bags of coffee. It is six miles from São Vicente, the former capital of the state of São Paulo. São Vicente was first settled in 1532.

I woke up at dawn and went to the deck of the ship. It had already docked. I looked all around. The harbor was deserted except for a lone black man forcing himself to walk aimlessly. I felt a sudden bang in my heart as if I was realizing the seriousness of the situation. I thought, "Here I am with a wife and four children depending on me, with very little money and no job waiting for me, in a foreign country whose language I can't even speak." I was interrupted in my train of thought by the first mate, who wished me jovially a good morning and then said, "I know exactly how you feel. Please don't get discouraged. Luck will smile at you. You have a very nice family. Don't fail them now when they need you most." Those encouraging words made me recover my self-confidence and I felt like waking up from a nightmare. I thanked the first mate for his encouragement, and told him that I already felt better.

That morning the passengers were served an early breakfast. They were lined up next to the dining room by eight o'clock. The health and immigration authorities took their places at two large separate tables at an angle from each other. The passengers were first processed by the health authorities; they then moved to the table occupied by the immigration officers. These latter checked their documents and stamped their passports, to prove that the passport holder was a legal immigrant in Brazil. My family's health and immigration formalities were completed by eleven o'clock. I took my place in the line, to have our baggage examined by the customs officers. It was time for our baby's milk bottle. Steffi and the children left to look for a place to get milk for the baby and some snacks and refreshments for themselves. Shortly before twelve noon, a customs officer moved along the line, gave us a number, and told us to come back at three p.m. after the lunch break (12–3 p.m.) I went with my family to a restaurant, where they had their snack. Steffi told me, as she could not speak Portuguese, the language spoken in Brazil, that she pointed to the baby with the empty milk bottle and said, "Milk." The waiter laughed, saying, "Leite quente," warm milk. She thus learned two important words in Portuguese.

It was six o'clock p.m. by the time we were through with the customs inspection. We still had to get to São Paulo. A German-speaking travel agent tried to sell us a station wagon to take us to São Paulo. We did not bite. Some English-speaking people, who had come to welcome fellow passengers, advised us to leave our heavy bales in the customs store for safekeeping, to which newly arrived immigrants were entitled a month free of charge, then to carry our personal luggage to downtown Santos in a streetcar and catch a bus to São Paulo. We followed their advice. We went downtown accompanied by Father John who unceremoniously attached himself to us. At the bus depot we found out that a bus to São Paulo had left a few minutes before. However, there were other buses that left the depot every hour on the hour. We were relieved at the news. Being hungry and tired, we went to the next-door Bar and Restaurant. Sailors of the Moore-McGormick line that plies between New York and Brazil were having drinks at the bar. One of the sailors came to our table when he heard us speaking English. He volunteered to help us when he heard our story. He said, "Let us first get the remainder of your luggage from the customs store, to go with you in the same bus." In his company, we hired a cab, recovered our excess luggage, delivered it to the bus depot and we were back at the restaurant within forty-five minutes. The same sailor also helped us to convert some of our dollars into local currency (cruseiros) at a much better rate of exchange. We enjoyed a leisurely meal with Brazilian beer before boarding the bus to São Paulo. We will never forget the kindness of the sailors of the Moore-McGormick line.

São Paulo

It was nearly one o'clock after midnight when we reached the city of São Paulo. The cab driver we hired stopped at three different hotels in search of accommodation for us. We were offered a large room with enough beds for all to share. We were forced to accept, having no other choice. Father John took a bed in a corner behind a portable partition. Our family occupied beds scattered in different parts of the room.

In the morning, Steffi went to the post office to claim the mail that we expected to be addressed, "Poste Restante, São Paulo, Brazil," the international way of addressing mail to travelers with no fixed address. All our friends and relatives were requested to address letters to us in this fashion.

When living in Bethlehem, Jordan, before 1967, and later in Beirut, Lebanon, there was no postal or mail service between the Arab countries and Israel, the same as at the present time. The Arab states do not recognize the State of Israel. We had friends in different European consulates; they moved freely between Israel and the Arab countries. They were glad to carry letters from us to our relatives in Jerusalem, Israel, and also letters from them to us. "Who is smarter, the authorities or the folk?" We sent massive letters to Israel through Athens post office, informing our relatives of our migration. We sent more letters from Genoa, Italy; Marseilles, France; and Barcelona, Spain.

Steffi came back from the post office carrying a big bag full of mail. I had promised Father John to accompany him to the convent of his order in Santo Amaro, a suburb of São Paulo. There he would refund us the money we had spent on him. We left after a quick breakfast. Steffi was happy to be left with the large correspondence she had gotten from the post office. The children were all busy with the letters they received from friends and grandparents.

Father John and I were welcomed in Santo Amaro. I was invited to have lunch with the Father Superior and his priests. There was no mention of Father John's expenses. I took leave of the religious community of Santo Amaro, Father John accompanied me to the bus. On the way he promised to send me the money from Bahia, northern Brazil, where he would be stationed. Steffi was all excited and had good news for me on my return to the hotel. Her mother had written that she had a cousin in São Paulo, Dr. Fritz Ottensooser. He was a professor at the university, and she sent his address. Steffi called Bertha, his wife, on the phone, she came to the hotel, and they had an encouraging visit. I mentioned what happened in Santo Amaro. She said, "We can forget the money, we should consider helping Father John as a good deed. We shall never hear from him. You at least had a free lunch." We never heard from Father John.

In the early 1930s, my cousin Archak, son of Aunt Masrur, oldest sister of my mother, was helped by my father to migrate to Brazil. In a letter from my mother, she gave us his business address in São Paulo. Archak had gone to Brazil from Jerusalem with his best friend. Shortly after they got settled, they opened a shoe factory in São Paulo. Incidentally, a large number of Armenian immigrants in Brazil are owners of shoe factories. They proudly announce that the Armenian shoe factories are the reason that the Brazilians go barefoot no more. Archak was a very trusting person. He managed the production and his friend took care of the finances. The factory was progressing nicely when his friend and partner absconded with the cash reserve, leaving Archak holding the bag with the factory liabilities. Archak was forced to declare bankruptcy. He ended up managing a shoe factory for another Armenian. I went to see Archak on our second day in São Paulo. He was very happy to see me and introduced me to his boss. He took the day off to help me get oriented in the strange city. We first went to see the parish priest, Father Gabriel, who as I mentioned before, knew my family from Jerusalem, where he was stationed, and had baptized our son Joseph Sebastian. I asked for his help in finding a house to live in. He said that should not be difficult, and told me to come back at two p.m. when he would have some news for me.

I was back in time after I had lunch with my cousin. Father Gabriel had good news. He had called an Armenian landlord in Tucuruvi, a suburb of São Paulo, who was expecting us. We arrived at his villa at three p.m. The landlord, Mr. Kevorkian, came from a well-known Armenian Catholic family in Marash, a city in Turkish Armenia. He survived by a miracle the Turkish massacre of the Armenians during World War I. He migrated to Brazil with the help of the Catholic Church. He began selling neckties made by his wife and daughters. He had to bite the bullet for some time. He is now a well-to-do landlord, with a son in an elective office in the state government, and a second son, an officer, graduated from the Federal Brazilian Military Academy. Mr. Kevorkian was a very pleasant and gracious host. A servant offered us delicious fruit juices freshly squeezed from fruits of the villa's orchard, also golden papaya ripened on the trees, picked up that same morning and cooled in the refrigerator. Our host, said, "In Brazil, papaya is called mamao (pronounced maman, the last syllable from the nose). The reason, as explained to me by a Portuguese acquaintance, is that a child walking with his mother was fascinated by the golden fruit on a tree. He tugged at his mother's skirt, shouting, mamao, mamao, pointing his finger at the fruit. The world used to get papaya from Africa, where a child accompanying his father noticed the golden fruit and shouted, papai, papai (father, father in Portuguese), pointing at the fruit. Well, this is only a Portuguese tale. You will hear quite a few of them while living in this country."

At this point, Father Gabriel tactfully brought up the purpose of our visit. Mr. Kevorkian offered us a two-bedroom house with a small garden, behind his villa, for rental on generous terms. We moved in the very next day, after buying some beds and the minimum requirement to start a new household. We had to be careful to spend as little as possible of the small amount of money we had. Our next stop was to get registered in the office for newly arrived immigrants, and get I.D. cards (Modelo Desanove) without which one could not get employment in Brazil. As soon as we moved into the house, Steffi called Bertha, her new-found cousin, to give her the news and our address. Bertha, with her husband, lived in the swanky Avenida Paulista. She belonged to an exclusive bridge club, and represented her club in many international tournaments.

Getting Settled in São Paulo, Brazil

São Paulo is the capital of the State of São Paulo, most populated state of the Union (Estados Unidos do Brasil) comprising 21 states, five federal territories and a federal district containing the country's capital. It is the largest industrial center of the nation and was called "the Chicago of South America." It was founded on the river Tieté as an Indian settlement by the Jesuits under Manuel de Nobrega in 1554, the anniversary of the conversion of St. Paul. It succeeded São Vicente as capital of the captaincy in 1681 and was elevated to city status in 1711. As the most populous city, São Paulo is supplied with power by a huge hydroelectric plant built in Cubatão on the way to Santos. The city is just within the tropics and has high temperatures in summer. It is on a plateau at an elevation of 2,400 feet and it thus has a temperate climate with some freezing days in winter.

We had reached São Paulo on a Monday. We were living in our new home by Thursday. I went to the American Chamber of Commerce on Friday to look for a job. The American Chamber of Commerce, to which most of the industries belong, issues a weekly business-news bulletin to its members. In a section of the bulletin, the jobs available are reported, also qualifications of job seekers.

I was interviewed by the editor of the bulletin; he said that the bulletin for the current week was already out. He would make some phone calls; he asked me to return on Monday and he might have some news for me. I reported to him on Monday; he said, "The Eveready branch of the Union Carbide Corporation is located one floor above. They need a person capable of doing English correspondence—does it interest you?" I said, "I will give

Jacob Orfali   55

it a try." I climbed to the next floor with a note given to me addressed to Mr. John Blount, manager of Eveready, which I presented to Mr. Blount with a copy of my summary. He read the summary and said, "Very impressive, but can you write English correspondence?" I answered, "I did it in my different jobs." He asked me to write a letter to their company's plant manager in Hong Kong to draw his attention to some discrepancy in the latest shipment to Brazil. I addressed my letter and began writing. He stopped me after the first paragraph, saying, "I see you are fluent in English correspondence. I would like to hire you, if you agree to work for 5,000 cruseiros a month." I accepted the offer and I reported to work the next day. Mr. Blount's secretary introduced me to the general manager, then the department heads and fellow workers. Except for the managers, who were Americans, all other personnel were Brazilians. The desk on my right was occupied by Paul, the company purchaser, a very sociable young man of British origin. He served in the R.A.F. during World War II. Paul was helping with the English correspondence in addition to his purchasing job. He was relieved of the correspondence when it started to interfere with his other duties. He spoke Portuguese like a native and considered himself Brazilian.

Most of the important South American industries were controlled by foreign capital, even the utilities such as water supply, natural gas, electricity, the streetcars, the railway, etc. British companies had the lion's share. The companies sent people from the home office to manage their business; most of them were married and brought their wives with them. Their children were born and grew up in the country where their fathers worked: they felt allegiance to the native country, and not more than lukewarm sympathy to their parents' country. Times were changing; more foreign industries, especially the utilities, were being taken over by Brazilians. According to the new laws, all businesses in Brazil were to have at least 51% Brazilian ownership. Japanese companies were also gaining inroads in business. They acquired virgin land, and operated very successful agricultural cooperatives.

I considered my job with the Union Carbide as a first step for a better future position, while studying Portuguese diligently. I corresponded mainly with the Hong Kong plant, source of the Eveready manufactured products. Though financed by U.S dollars, payments for goods shipped to Brazil were made in sterling pounds which were more easily obtainable than U.S. dollars.

Sometime in the middle of my first work week, as I got home, I noticed that the walkway leading to the garden in the back of the house was piled up with good quality furniture. All kinds of dressers, cupboards, tables, chairs, etc. were blocking the way. Steffi came out of the house, bursting with happiness. It seemed that our newly discovered cousin Bertha had talked about our family to her friends. One of her friends decided to buy new furniture. She sent a truckload of all the replaced furniture to our address. It confirmed our belief that such people of good will do really exist.

I progressed very nicely in my work, in a pleasant atmosphere. My colleagues helped me in my effort to learn Portuguese. Our son George was enrolled in a high school near our house, and daughter Gabrielle was accepted in a nun's private school. George also worked a few hours a day after school in the municipal market helping one of the merchants. Joseph Sebastian went to a small preparatory school in the house of a private teacher. The teacher kept repeating the same lesson (in Portuguese). It read, "A bata nada," the duck swims, again and again. Joseph got fed up with the swimming duck after a while. He said one day that he wanted to kill the duck and proceed to learn other things. We knew the so-called school was too loud and overcrowded. Joseph was at least with other children of his age and if nothing else, he was exposed to the Portuguese language. We decided to keep him there.

I received a reply to a complaint I had addressed to the head-quarters of the Messageries Maritime in France about their giving us lousy accommodations on the S.S. Florida instead of a family cabin which was paid for. The company management apologized for the misunderstanding and sent us a check to compensate for the monetary difference. It was not much, but every little bit helped. Christmas was nearing. I received a formal letter from the management of the Union Carbide inviting me to a party on Christmas Eve, in a nice restaurant where the employees used to get their noon meals. Employees bought coupons for a nominal price, for which they got a full meal at the restaurant—a company fringe benefit. During the party, we talked about personal matters. I spoke about my life experiences and what made us come to Brazil. The general manager distributed presents, and special ones for each child of the employees. We were planning no Christmas celebration, but things changed when a colleague of German origin drove me home with the packages of company presents. George had brought home a Christmas tree from the market, and we decorated the tree with candles and knick-knacks we had brought with us that were used in past Christmasses. In the evening, we lit the candles, sang Christmas carols, and enjoyed a family dinner. The Christmas presents were opened and engendered happy exclamations. We passed our Christmas day with my cousin Archak and family; he had invited us for dinner. Archak was married to a Brazilian lady of Portuguese descent and they had five very nice children, three daughters and two sons. We spent a very pleasant time, with the children getting acquainted and the grown-ups reminiscing. We were well content upon going to bed on Christmas night. I meditated for a while before surrendering to the arms of Morpheus (sleep). I thought that we just celebrated the birth of the greatest Innovator the world has ever known. For lack of decent living quarters, His mother Mary gave birth to Him in a stable. For the absence of a cradle, Mary placed her newborn infant on straw in a manger. He got warmed by the breath of animals. When He grew up, the Prince of Peace preached peace and compassion. His followers have spread His teachings to mankind all over the world for the last two thousand years. People seem to be deaf, indifferent to the cries of the needy and blind to the sufferings of their own neighbors. Millions of hungry children cry themselves to sleep every night. Those who could afford to help are unmoved. Greed and pride, causes of all evil, are the order of the day. May the Almighty have mercy on us, and protect us from the consequences.

Finally Settled in São Paulo

A company secretary caught up with me on my way to lunch a few days after Christmas. She brought up the conversation we had at the Christmas party. "At the party you spoke about the interminable lines waiting for a bus to take people home after work," and then she said, "You also mentioned that you taught foreign languages, right?" I said, "Right."

Lucia, the secretary, said, "I have a suggestion profitable to all concerned. I talked over your teaching foreign languages with fellow employees. As their representative, I request you to consider teaching us English, 45–60 minutes twice a week after work. We have the company's approval to meet in the conference room. We will be fifteen pupils, and will pay you ten cruseiros each for every lesson. You will earn our eternal gratitude for your help, and shorten the time two days a week that we wait in line for a bus in rush hour." I agreed to the request and the secretary volunteered to do the required typing involved. We began the lessons the next Monday; they proceeded smoothly in a relaxed atmosphere. Everybody had fun, crowned with speedy good results. The earning of an additional 1,200 cruseiros a month improved our budget substantially. It took less time to catch a bus after the rush hour. Incidentally, tropical rain fell exactly at five o'clock every day for about one hour, just the time when all offices closed. Rainfall never failed at that time; people made appointments to meet after the rain.

Hans, the young man of German origin who gave me a ride with the Christmas party presents, had a pleasant surprise for me in January. I had mentioned to him during the ride that I brought with me some Persian rugs which I bought in Beirut as an investment. I was ready to start selling them. He said, "I would like to buy one of your rugs, as a present for my aunt's birthday." I was happy to make a deal with him. He picked up the rug next day.

He got a bargain, I received urgently needed cash.

At dinnertime one night, my son George said, "Dad, I met Maria, a Russian lady. She is the school janitress. She is married to Grisha, an Armenian shoe repairman—his store is next to our school. He wants very much to meet you." I said, "He will soon have his own shoe factory like the other Armenians. I will go and see him on my day off, next Saturday." Grisha or Gregory (Krikor in Armenian) was one of the many thousands of slave workers relocated to Germany when the Nazis invaded their country. They replaced the conscripted German workers in the industries. Some of the slave workers had wives and children from whom they were forcibly separated. A few of these married persons met new mates and started a family. At the end of the war (World War II), the slave workers became "displaced persons," and they refused to go back to their country of origin. The victorious allies, mostly the U.S.A., solved the problem of displaced persons by transporting them to countries accepting immigrants. Grisha, an Armenian, and Maria, a Russian, two displaced persons, met in Germany; they got married and had a daughter. They were brought to Brazil in an American ship with thousands of persons with the same status. All displaced persons were provided with cash to help them start a new life. They were given privileges by the country of immigration, such as tax exemptions and trade facilities.

Brazil had moving markets or feiras. The participating merchants transported their goods in trucks they owned themselves or in partnership with other merchants. They were assigned permanent spots where they displayed their merchandise on stands or tables, in the feira, in a different suburb every day of the week, Saturdays and Sundays included. After gaining experience, many of them moved to other trades. New immigrants with no skills usually tried their luck in the feiras, where they at least learned to speak Portuguese.

We became friendly with Grisha's family; during our visits they talked about their experiences as slave workers in Germany, their deprivations and hardships. They spoke of the problems of those who were forced to abandon their families back home, now with new mates and children. They were considered dead by their country of birth and their families enjoyed special privileges as survivors of heroes who died for the fatherland. Those who went back to their families were arrested by the authorities and prosecuted for treason.

We took trips to surrounding recreation areas on our days off. George joined the Tieté nautical club, took fencing lessons in addition to other sports activities. He took us for a cruise in a boat provided by his club, on the Tieté River. We visited a virgin forest and contemplated with awe the natural growth of the most exquisite orchids on majestic trees. We went to Butanta snake farm, a world-famous center for the study of snakes, production of antitoxins and antivenins. We did not feel the passage of time. We made local friends, and participated in their social activities. We spoke Portuguese fluently without feeling how it happened. We had our first taste of Brazilian Carnival before Ash Wednesday. Carnival is the period of feasting and having fun before Lent. It begins on Saturday night of the week before Lent and ends on the morning of Ash Wednesday. The broadcasting stations play samba music, new hits competing for first place, and continuous parties go on in private clubs. The main thoroughfares are crowded with costumed people singing and dancing.

Promenading crowds squirt each other with cheap perfume from a special sprayer, "lanca perfume" carried by the crowd. The big parade of floats in São Paulo takes place in Avenidas São-Joao, the largest avenue downtown, where the different colleges of samba display the result of many hours of creative work, when they compete for first prize. The monetary prizes consist of city contributions to the winning units, to be used for next year's Carnival floats. A very vigilant public security maintains order, rowdies and drunks are taken to jail where they are kept until noon of Ash Wednesday. A big crowd assembles at the entrance of city jail on that day. Those arrested during Carnival are freed at midday, 12 o'clock sharp, when they are greeted with loud jeers, catcalls, and hand-clapping by the waiting crowd.

Changing Jobs

I had just completed my eleventh month with Eveready when the secretary of the American Chamber of Commerce introduced me to a gentleman by the name of John Hanson from Boston, Massachusetts. He was the personnel manager of a branch of an international construction company. The São Paulo Light and Power Company contracted them to build a thermoelectric generating plant. Mr. Hanson said that he had read my summary and would like to make me an offer for a job fit for my work experience. He asked me how much I would be willing to work for, to change jobs. I said, "I have to have 12,000 monthly." Mr. Hanson replied, "I understand you are making 5,000 cruseiros now—how about 7,000 cruseiros?" I declined his offer. He urged me to go and see Mr. Erik Olson, the company plant controller in Pedreira, a few miles from Santo Amaro. I was grilled in an interview by Mr. Olson. He must have been impressed and offered me 9,000 cruseiros. I insisted on 12,000 cruseiros, but finally settled for 10,000.

I reported to the Pedreira construction site at the expiration of the seven days' notice I gave to Eveready. I began by training new employees for the comptroller. My official title was Cost Engineer. My boss, the chief Cost Engineer, had not yet arrived from Boston. I kept the general ledger and performed accounting work while waiting. At the arrival of my boss, we moved to a new office and hired three more helpers whom I trained and supervised. My day began with site inspection of the construction the first thing in the morning. I took note of the progress of work, the percentage completed as against the total to be done. I checked the daily progress report of labor and material and compiled the actual cost and compared it with the cost estimate. In case of differences, the engineer in charge was asked for an explanation.

One day after a heavy tropical rain, we had a near-insurrection in Pedreira. The field construction engineer in charge stormed into the office of the general manager, shouting, "I am not going to tolerate this any more! How do you expect me to get work out of a half-starved, improperly dressed, bare-footed crew? I insist on paying them enough wages to buy themselves proper clothes. They should also be issued rubber boots and raincoats by tomorrow. Unless you want me to take the next plane home!" The wages were set by Brazilian regulations which the company had to obey according to the Brazilian personnel manager. The general manager came to terms with the labor department, which made an exception in that the company's laborers would be paid higher wages than the maximum allowed by law. The laborers got higher wages in addition to boots and raincoats. They also did an excellent job.

I stayed with this job for two years. The representatives of the São Paulo Light and Power came to inspect the plant that was soon ready to be handed over to them. The chief engineer of the client company, "São Paulo Light and Power Company," offered me a job as assistant to the vice president of the engineering department with a higher salary. I could not refuse.

My Ideal Job

The São Paulo Light and Power Company, also known as the Brazilian Traction, had a concession to build power plants to produce and sell electric power in Brazil. I was now inspecting the progress of all the plants under construction, comparing actual cost against estimate and reporting to my boss the contractors' excuses for any discrepancy. I traveled to the construction sites close to São Paulo in a chauffeured car, and ordered air travel and hotel accommodations through the company's personnel department. I had an unlimited pre-approved expense account.

We Acquire a Bar

In the meantime, we went through what could be compared to a nightmare. An immigrant family from Bethlehem came to see us. They had presents for us from my Aunt Justine, who is a nun in that city. Mr. George Butros told me he was interested in buying a bar to earn a living. It so happened that we knew of a bar for sale near our house. It was owned by an old Lebanese man ready to retire. I helped him to make a deal, and without thinking, signed the agreement as guarantor. It turned out that Mr. Butros had no reserve money and could not meet his obligations. We got stuck with a bar that we did not need. My wife and children took charge; they operated it with the help of an experienced employee. Our family life was disrupted; what would have been leisure time for us was taken up by work in the bar. The only family meal we had together was on Sunday when the bar was closed from one to four p.m. The worst part was that instead of making money, we invested everything we had in the bar. We were very relieved when a newly arrived family from Portugal bought the bar, though we lost money in the deal.

In the meantime, Joseph Sebastian was smuggled into a school near our house by a teacher we knew; she made arrangements with a first-grade teacher to include him on the list of her pupils. It was impossible to enroll him otherwise in the school near our house, and it did not hurt anybody to bypass the red tape. Johnny, our youngest, spoke Portuguese fluently, but no other language. Our other children spoke German or English, but Johnny communicated with us in Portuguese only. He was a very happy child and was loved and spoiled by everybody. A disc jockey was our best customer and a good friend of ours. He lived next to our bar with his wife. They had no children, and Johnny was more in their house than in the bar when Steffi replaced the hired helper. They fed him, bathed him, and let him have his afternoon nap in a private room. He entertained the customers dancing the samba when he was not carried by one of our regular customers. Joseph Sebastian's best friend was the son of a Japanese neighbor; he often accompanied his friend to a Japanese school and learned about Japanese customs and children's tales. He told us about some of these.

Our daughter Gabrielle was the quiet type who did what she was told without complaint. She was a big help to her mother and a good companion. She did well at school and had many Brazilian girl friends.

We were now free to renew contact with friends. Steffi joined me every Thursday in the home of Dr. Fritz and his wife Bertha, where I went after work to help the doctor in translating his research papers into English. We had dinner together and visited afterwards. We belonged to the German Catholic community of São Paulo; our son Joseph Sebastian followed instructions there when he prepared for his first communion. It was too far for us to go to Mass there every Sunday (we had to take a bus to town and a second bus from town to the German community center). We went to Mass in a church of our neighborhood. We attended the important meetings of the German community.

The São Paulo German Catholic community wanted to be represented in the International Eucharistic Congress in Rio de Janeiro. We joined the group that went to the Federal Capital that was still at Rio de Janeiro at that time, to participate in the events of the Congress. The whole college of Cardinals had come and we witnessed unforgettable ceremonies with pomp and pageantry at a large open-air altar especially created for the occasion. We attended a Mass celebrated by the German Cardinal and a second one celebrated by the Armenian Cardinal Aghajanian in the famous church of Our Lady of Candelaria, with its twin towers and graceful dome. Cardinal Aghajanian would have been elected Pope, had he been Italian. We were conveyed to the Sugar Loaf Mountain (Pão de Açúcar), the conical rock rising 1,296 feet above the water level. We had already been at the Corcovado (Hunchback) a 98-1/2–foot statue of Christ the Redeemer, erected on the peak of a 2,310 foot rock above the Botafogo inlet, when we first stopped in Rio de Janeiro on our way to Santos. We returned home with a feeling of fulfillment, having enjoyed every minute of our trip.

On another occasion, we took the pilgrimage bus to Nossa Senhora Apparecida on the way to Rio de Janeiro, where a black wooden statue found in the river is venerated. Miraculous healings are credited to the wooden statue. It was a very interesting day's excursion; our children enjoyed being wondered at as natives of the holy land.

Officially the majority of the people living in Brazil were Roman Catholic. Some are Roman Catholic in name only. They are inside a church first at baptism, then when they get married, and finally after they die and their body is brought to church for the funeral Mass. There was a time when Catholics only were admitted as immigrants into South American countries. That is no more. Nobody asked about our religion in the Brazilian embassy in Beirut where we got our immigration visas. The immigrants coming with us in the ship included Greek Orthodox, Protestants, Jews, etc. Many Mormon, Baptist, and other protestant churches as well as Greek Orthodox churches and synagogues operate freely in Brazil and they have large communities. Father Gabriel came to bless our house once a year, and every time we changed homes. It is an ancient tradition practiced in the old country. In Jerusalem, it took the parish priest a whole week to bless the homes of the parishioners.

We got accustomed to the taste of pinga, or caxassa (cashassa), the national drink of the common Brazilians. It is made of distilled juice of sugarcane. It is drunk straight or mixed with crushed lime and sugar called caipirinha (caypirinia), also as rabo do galo (cock tail) mixed with vermouth. We joined our newly acquired friends and neighbors, partook of these drinks at parties and festival occasions. One of the popular celebrations was the feast of São-João (St. John) on June 21 or 22, date of the winter solstice, when the days start getting longer. Homemade balloons cover the sky at night; they are made of cloth carrying a lit candle or rugs soaked in fuel suspended on strings tied on the cloth. The heat from the candles or fuel under the cloth causes it to rise like a balloon. Some balloons fall on the roofs of houses and start fires; it keeps firemen busy. The celebrations are in the fields around large open fires, with drinking, singing, and dancing in each neighborhood.

Citizens of former colonies feel smarter than those living in the mother country. They poke fun at them and tell jokes about their immaturity.

Here are some jokes I heard about Portuguese immigrants.

Manuel and Paulo reach Rio de Janeiro from Portugal a few days before Christmas. In the evening they walk in the city park; the trees are decorated with multicolored electric lights. Manuel tells Paulo he will return soon to Portugal. Paulo urges Manuel to tell the reason. Manuel says, "I will leave as soon as I buy seeds or plants of these light trees to grow in Portugal." On another occasion, Manuel sees a parrot and he stops and looks at him with fascination. The parrot says, "Bon dia amigo," (good morning, friend) to him. Manuel is all confused, he says, "Desculpe senhor, eu pensava que o senhor era ave," (Excuse me, sir, I thought you were a bird). I guess the reader gets the idea.

Our son George graduated from high school at the end of the 1956 school year. Unlike the United States, young unmarried people are not allowed to meet their dates without chaperons. Steffi and I accompanied George and his date, a secretary from my office, to the graduation party. George got a job in the office of a big department store; he liked the job and his boss liked him, and promised him a good future in the company. That was not what we were planning for our children. Higher education in Brazil was very expensive; besides that, the universities were overcrowded. Only children of influential people were accepted. We had neither the money nor the required influence. I was toying with the idea of emigrating to the United States. I had even made inquiries at the American Consulate, where I was told that as my wife was born in Germany, we only had to be sponsored by an American citizen and we would get our immigration permit or visa upon presentation of the affidavit.

Previously families were separated, the member born in a country that had a vacancy in its unfilled quota was allowed to enter the U.S.A., and the remaining members of the family followed later upon fulfilling certain conditions. President Eisenhower changed the law that was causing hardship to families through long separations. The new law said that as long as one member of the family satisfies the requirements, the whole family is admitted as immigrants on the quota of his or her country. Every country is allowed a certain quota of immigrants to enter the U.S.A., on a first-come, first-served basis. No more immigration visas or permits are issued in a certain year when the quota is filled. New applicants have to wait for the quota of the following year. It so happened that there were few applicants for the German quota when we applied. The children were very delighted when I brought up the subject of emigrating to the U.S.A., but Steffi was not as enthusiastic. She said, "Now that we've settled down at last and made some good friends, the idea of moving again does not appeal to me."

I had heard of George Mardikian, a famous Armenian restaurateur in San Francisco, who was a well-known philanthropist. President Eisenhower, who was his friend, asked him to visit the military camps at home and overseas, to help improve the quality of food consumed by the armed services. He was decorated for his success. George Mardikian was at the head of an Armenian organization helping Armenians in distress to immigrate to the United States. I wrote to him and described my situation. I mentioned my deceased uncle's name (John Haig) who was his friend, and requested him to help my family relocate in the United States. He told me that the organization would be happy to help. I should first write to my uncle's widow, who would be offended if they helped John's nephew without her knowledge. Aunt Hozanna is the second wife of my Uncle John. She was manager of his knitting factory. He married her shortly before he passed away. I had never corresponded with her. I went to the library of U.S.I.S. (United States Information Service) and looked for the name Haig in the telephone directory of Chicago. There were a few of them. I copied the address that sounded plausible to me. I sent my letter to that address. I received her reply promptly; she asked the names, place and date of birth of the members of my family needed for the affidavit, and the cash amount needed for the travel. I sent her the information and begged for a loan of $5,000. She sent the affidavit and $5,000 within two weeks. By now, Steffi had reconciled to the idea of emigrating to the United States. She studied the cost of travel offered by different agencies; having helped her father in this travel agency, she was familiar with what is involved. On her advice, it was decided to travel by cargo ship. Though slow, it was cheaper than flying (in which case, we would have to pay extra for the luggage). It would also give us a well-deserved vacation. When I resigned from my job, my boss tempted me to stay by offering me more money, to no avail. We boarded the S.S. Del Monte in Santos with my cousin and a delegation of friends who came to see us off. We had our last celebration in Brazil with a farewell party aboard the ship.

Stephanie Orfali on board the ship S.S. Del Monte

Chapter 8.

Moving to the USA

The S.S. Del Monte

The S.S. Del Monte belonged to the Del Line with headquarters in New Orleans, our port of entry to the Untied States. We were assigned a large family cabin with bathroom and toilet. The only other passenger was a young Argentinian missionary priest on his way to China: he was to replace American priests who were no longer welcome in China. The ship weighed anchor in the middle of the night, and we were on the way to Rio de Janeiro for loading cargo. We had breakfast with the captain surrounded by the officers next morning before we reached Rio.

We went ashore for a last farewell visit to Rio de Janeiro. It was Tuesday before Ash Wednesday; we watched some Carnival floats and returned to the ship before dark. Next morning, the ship docked at the port of Vitoria, capital city of the state of Espirito Santo in the bay of the same name. The entrance to the bay is tortuous and rather difficult, but it is deep enough for large vessels. We passed the hull of a Dutch sunken ship on the way to the port. The city is spread around the bay. It is connected by a rickety railway which we took, not knowing what we were getting into. I was going to buy some gems as investments in São Paulo. (Some friends who knew the ship would stop at Victoria advised me to buy them in that city, where they are much cheaper.) I bought some aquamarine, amethyst, and topaz cut stones through the bank in Vitoria, while the ship was unloading and loading cargo.

Our last stop was at Fortaleza, a city and port of northern Brazil, capital of the state of Ceara. The name Ceara is derived from the Arabic word of Sahra, which means desert. It is also the origin of the word "Sahara." The Portuguese and Spanish languages contain many words of Arabic origin, due to the Arabic occupation of the Iberian peninsula for seven hundred years. The climate is arid in this region; the high temperature is modified by the strong sea winds. We enjoyed watching the jangadas (sailrafts) speeding in the Atlantic. Before leaving the shores of Brazil, let me mention that the main staple of the country is arroz-feijão (rice and beans). On Sundays, spaghetti is added. No meal is complete without rice and beans.

After Fortaleza, a steel cable towline was dropped into the ocean. It had a hook at its end with some bait and was attached to an alarm on the ship. A few days later, the alarm sounded, and everybody rushed to the back of the ship to watch a huge marlin being hauled aboard. Part of it was served in a meal, it tasted delicious. The ship continued northward at a steady speed; we could see schools of fish in the ocean. Flying fish had fun crossing from one side of the ship to the other, a few of them did not make it; they collided with each other in mid-air, thus littering the deck. We detected water currents traversing the ocean; one could see them with the naked eye, especially the Gulf Stream, which was really fast. We got used to the routine, went for a stroll on the deck, chatted with the crew, went through the books of the ship's small library. Unless we joined the Captain with the off-duty officers at eight A.M., we breakfasted whenever we felt like it. The refrigerator was stuffed with all kinds of gourmet food and we were told that we should feel free to help ourselves at any time. Hot drinks were always available in large thermos containers. We got better acquainted with the young priest: he told us that he would spend some time in his Order's convent in Illinois, to meet former missionaries and get their advice. The ship's Captain and officers went out of their way to make us feel comfortable. We spoke French with the second mate, who claimed French ancestry. We played poker with him and he taught us different variations of the game; we learned the Down-the-River version while sailing up the river in the gulf toward New Orleans. No alcoholic drinks were obtainable at the ship's store, crew members and passengers buying their requirements on land before leaving. We appreciated the invitations to the first mate's cabin, where he served us cocktails. The first mate was Acadian—Acadians are descendants of the French settlers of Acadia, a French colony in eastern Canada which became English by the Treaty of Utrecht in 1713 at the defeat of the French by the English. The Acadians were forcibly deported into different English colonies, which inspired Longfellow's *Evangeline*. One group of Acadians found its way to Bayou Teche, Louisiana. George Washington Cable describes their subsequent life in the Bayou.

We were processed speedily by the immigration officers in New Orleans before landing. They told Johnny jokingly that he would be sent back to Brazil because he couldn't speak English. Poor Johnny was downcast and did not know how to react. He gave a big smile resembling the sun bursting through dark clouds when told it was a joke. I mentioned the gems we bought in Vitoria on the customs declaration form, and the customs authorities did not search our luggage. The second mate promised to meet us at the hotel St. Charles. He came late in the afternoon and drove us around to introduce us to American life the Louisiana way. He drove through the French quarter, which is settled by Italians from New York, and we saw some blacks with saxophones playing nostalgic melodies on street corners, as well as a marching band of youngsters practicing Mardi Gras music. We had steak dinner at Joe's renowned restaurant.

Next day we visited the three sisters' well, then drove to the famous suburb of Maiteri and saw the 25,000-foot bridge across Lake Ponchatrain. When we sat at the end of the bus, people gazed at us as if we had horns. It was later explained to us that white folks didn't sit in the back with black people. This sounded really strange; there had been no segregation in Brazil.

We took the interstate train to Chicago. I was having a drink at the bar, and the waiter urged me to finish it up as we were nearing a dry state. It seemed that the bar was supposed to close every time we were nearing a dry state where it was illegal to serve alcohol. The train stopped suddenly at night on the middle of a bridge; all the lights went off and we could hear a torrential rain falling in the river under us. There was lightning and thunder, then a complete silence as the frogs began croaking, and all kinds of scary thoughts crossed our minds. Suddenly the lights came on, the train started moving again, and we took a deep breath of relief.

We reached Chicago after the long, tiresome train ride. Aunt Hozanna, who had sponsored our immigration to the USA, with daughter and son-in-law, welcomed us in the central station. We were greeted by a snowfall outside the station. We had last seen snow on the Lebanese mountains in a forest of cedars five years before. They drove us in two cars to Aunt Hozanna's home. Her daughter's family (husband, son, and two daughters) lived in the lower floor of the house. Aunt Hozanna offered us the upper part, where she lived. We looked for a place to rent the next day. We found an apartment in the northwest part of town. Aunt Hozanna helped us buy good sturdy furniture from her supplier; it withstood many years of rough treatment, moving into five different houses during our twenty-two years' stay in Illinois.

I met many friends of my deceased uncle. One of them was a retired Justice of the Peace. He took me to the Abbott Laboratories in North Chicago (a pharmaceutical industry) and introduced me to the retired president who had an office on the premises. This gentleman arranged a cost accountant's job for me in the engineering department. I began commuting on a train from Chicago to my jobsite, a distance of forty miles each way. We later moved to Winthrop Harbor, one mile from the Wisconsin state line on Lake Michigan and eight miles from North Chicago. One of the engineers of Abbott Labs lived in Winthrop Harbor. I rode with him to and from work. Sometimes I drove my car. I took to the job as a duck to water, as the saying goes. The company had many fringe benefits: it had its own restaurant at the main building where employees got choices of different menus at very reasonable prices, plus free one-a-day vitamins. We could also buy medicine at a reduced price. Once a year, we had a family picnic with games for children and grown-ups, food, soft drinks, and coffee were provided free, and draft beer for minimal cost. I stayed with the Abbott Labs for over a year. In the meantime my sponsor, the old retired president, had passed away. We were in the 1958 recession: a nephew of one of the department heads may have needed a job; I was let go.

This reminds me of an appropriate joke. Three applicants for a vacancy in a bank were asked, "How much are two and two?" The first applicant answered, "Four." The second said, "It depends on the circumstances." The third applicant answered, "Five." Which one do you think got the job? I will tell you who. The bank president's nephew was always goofing off, getting into all kinds of mischief. His mother asked her bank president brother to give him a job. He was given the vacancy, and none of the applicants were hired.

We had rented the house in Winthrop Harbor from the owner's agent. The owner was transferred to Texas by his company. He did not want it rented, he wanted it sold. Consequently, we moved to Zion City, three miles south of Winthrop Harbor.

Jacob Orfali at work in the Post Office in Zion, Illinois

Chapter 9.

The City of Zion, Illinois

The Zion City (City of God) was envisioned by John Alexander Dowie, an Australian fundamentalist preacher who got his fame in Chicago where he had his ministry. He purchased over six thousand acres of farmland near Lake Michigan at the turn of the century. He was surrounded by equally dedicated persons; they created a city with biblical street names in the prairie farmland. Christians from all over the United States and foreign countries eagerly purchased land and relocated to the new city, to be near the charismatic preacher. A cooperative society was created, administered by the elders of the church which bore the name, "The Christian Catholic Church." The "Passion Play" performed by the local people outdoors was very famous and attracted many visitors to Zion. The Church felt obliged to build a hotel to accommodate the ever-increasing crowds. Expert lace workers were recruited and brought to Zion to teach the trade to gifted Zionites in a newly constructed lace factory. A curtain factory was already in operation; it specialized in custom draperies, supplied mainly through the Marshall Field stores of Chicago to their customers.

When we moved to Zion City in 1957, things had completely changed. In addition to a rival church that split from the Christian Catholic mother church, many Protestant denominational churches, as well as a Roman Catholic church, were in existence. The city fathers retained the original "dry" status (alcohol sale and consumption was prohibited in the city limits). Taverns and liquor stores a few hundred yards both north and south of the city limits did good business with customers from Zion. As a member of the Moose Club, half a mile north of Zion, I several times had drinks with an elder of the Christian Catholic Church and another elder of the rival church. The political affiliations of the faithful were influenced by the church to which he belonged. The elder of the Christian Catholic Church occupied a Republican-elected position; the elder of the rival church, a businessman who owned the local paper, was a Democrat.

The welcome-wagon lady came to see us in the first week we were in Zion. She gave us a few trinkets and lots of advertising material from the local merchants; she also arranged that our name be published in the local paper as new arrivals to Zion City. As a consequence of our name appearing in the paper, we received an unexpected visit from Peter, an elder of the Christian Catholic Church. We were in the Christian Brothers College together in Jerusalem. I had not seen him for over twenty-five years. He had joined the mentioned church at that time and was an ordained minister. The church helped him and his family to relocate to Zion City, where he was elected elder after a while. The church practiced divine healing. Peter was active in that line for the church. He visited mostly elderly ladies suffering from arthritis and "loneliness": he massaged their backs and shoulders, read a psalm with them, and gave them dry medicinal herbs to make tea (this is what he told me). I offered him a drink; he chose scotch from my collection of drinks.

Our two older children were enrolled in the Zion-Benton High School: George as senior, to get an American diploma and Gabrielle as a sophomore. Joseph Sebastian (Seb) went to grade school, and Johnny to Catholic parochial school.

On the first Sunday in Zion, we went to Mass at the Catholic church, and after Mass, we presented ourselves to the parish priest. We were shocked when, instead of asking about our credentials to register us in the parish book, he just stuck in my hand dated collection envelopes for the remaining weeks of the year. He then excused himself to attend to other church business. We expected some friendly talk, interest in our situation as new immigrants, etc., as is the custom practiced by parish priests in the Holy Land and Brazil, not this impersonal behavior.

Johnny's life at parochial school was not as pleasant as that of our other children in public school. It may partly have been due to Johnny's not being able to express himself in English. He was accused of other kids' mischief, which is known to happen in schools. The mother superior automatically punished Johnny without taking the trouble to investigate the veracity of the accusation. His teacher, a young Irish nun who liked Johnny, was very upset. She could not finger the real culprits—they were the mother superior's pets, children of good friends of hers. I went to see the parish priest about the matter, and he said that the school administration was outside his jurisdiction, under the Archdiocese of Chicago. I saw the mother superior myself and got no satisfaction. I asked for an appointment with the Archdiocese school administrator. He was a young, inexperienced priest. He must have been brainwashed by the mother superior of the parish school. Without giving me the chance to talk, he said, "Your son is a hood." I shouted back, "You know what you can do with the Zion parish school and its witch of a mother superior!" I went back home. Next day Johnny was enrolled in a public school, where he made good friends and was very happy. His school principal, Mr. Scaccia, was very nice to him and assigned him the privilege of raising and lowering the flag. It so happened that later on Mr. Scaccia's older son Frank married our daughter Gabrielle.

Many years later, I heard from a friend of the so-called mother superior that she had left the religious order and married the mayor of a small town near St. Louis, Missouri.

I had a very hard time finding a job in the recession period of 1958. The weekly unemployment compensation check did not amount to much. I had never heard of laying off salaried people before coming to the United States. It seemed that once you passed a certain age, companies were no longer interested in you, being under the impression that they couldn't train you to do things their way. As the saying goes, "There is the official way, the legal way, and the company way of doing a job." Unless I had help from the inside, someone who would vouch for me, no company seemed interested in hiring me. An old neighbor whom I had befriended advised me to join the political party of my choice, get active, devote many hours of my time, and I would be noticed by the right people. I would never be looking for a job.

After a while, I was hired as a machine operator by Johns Manville, in Waukegan, Illinois, five miles south of Zion, for the graveyard shift (midnight to eight A.M.) The personnel department sent me to the production manager with my résumé. This gentleman got off his chair after going through my papers, saying, "Here, you can get my job." I had never done factory work before, especially third shift; my body would not adjust to staying awake at night and sleeping in the daytime. I am mechanically gifted and I do not believe in goofing on the job. I found a way to do the work easier with increased production. The shop steward stopped at my machine one night with a message instructing me to report to Mr. Rawhide, the union labor contract negotiator. I paid a visit to Mr. Rawhide in the union hall next afternoon. He was very pleasant to talk to. He said it was reported to him that I was exceeding by far the production standard figure set by the company industrial engineers, and accepted by the labor-management contract. "I don't want to know how you do it—we know you are not cheating, your production figure is accurate. Neither the company management nor the union is happy about it. My request to you is to slow down. Please avoid problems to management and union by not exceeding the production standard."

Mr. Rawhide also represented the Democratic party in Zion; he spoke about his aim of building a strong Democratic constituency, as here only the Republicans were represented. I liked very much what I heard from him. I met him more often socially as time went by. I took an active part in the Democratic movement.

In the meantime, my wife Steffi, to help pay our expenses, got herself a job as a sewing machine operator in the sweat shop of the Zion Curtain Factory for the minimum wage of $1.00 an hour. After a year, Mr. Rawhide was called in by the workers to organize a union shop. A labor management agreement was signed raising the wages to $1.25 an hour with improved working conditions, and a yearly week's vacation. In retaliation, the company cancelled the morning coffee and sweet rolls, the Christmas turkey dinner with small presents (fringe benefits) it used to give the workers.

I was laid off when the work slowed down. I was employed in a thriving C.P.A.'s office twenty-five miles from Zion. I was progressing nicely when my car was struck on the highway by a high-school student who failed to obey a stop sign. I could not get to work for one month, and another applicant was hired in my place. My lawyer questioned a passenger traveling in the teenager's car, who admitted that he had seen my car and warned the driver to no avail. I won the case, but lost my job.

I went back to the factory, and this time I was hired as a quality control inspector. I worked for five years as inspector. I earned good wages, with lots of overtime. I was asked to inspect a rush order of pipes one day, every single pipe was way over the maximum average tolerance of the specifications. I rejected them. I refused to pass them despite the insistence of the production floor supervisor. I did the same thing when the production manager came accompanied by my boss. The production manager said, "The pipes will go underground, nobody could tell the difference." I did not budge. My boss gauged the pipes and shook his head with no comment. My honesty in this incident cost me my job, I was fired on trumped-up charges. I was exonerated in a labor court at which no company representative was present.

The citizens of Waukegan, Illinois, complained about the smoke of the factories' stacks causing inconvenience (hard breathing, headaches, etc.). The companies installed a special devise to divert the smoke into the working areas. The smoke was so thick at times that one could not see farther than five feet. I understand that factories still get away with such illegal acts, to save money, thus adding a few cents to the dividends of the shareholders.

In the meantime, the Democratic party recruiting of new members in Zion proceeded with good results. I donated my free time to the movement. We were now American citizens, and Steffi was

Jacob Orfali   81

teaching in a parochial school in Kenosha, Wisconsin, fifteen miles north of Zion. Steffi had consulted with the county superintendent of schools; he saw her Germany university credits (she was not allowed to continue her studies under the Nazi regime). The superintendent of schools encouraged her to take courses at night and get a job teaching parochial school. Of course, it was hard on her to take care of the family needs, hold a full-time job and go to school at night. Everybody pitched in to help make life easier. Steffi finally made it; hard work and dedication paid off. She taught public school after obtaining her teacher's certificate and taught German and French in high school. She was a guidance counselor with a master's degree when she retired from teaching.

I did my share of studying; I attended a special training for teachers, to teach religious courses to Catholics in public high schools. It was offered by the Confraternity of Christian Doctrine, to replace the old Catechism, as decided by the second ecumenical council, instigated by Pope John XXIII. In our parish, lay people were replaced by seminarians when the beloved Pope passed away. I was out of teaching

Steffi was also active in the Democratic movement. She became Democratic precinct committee captain. Our house hosted coffee parties for many Democrats running for office.

Our situation was not as desperate as when I lost my first job. I was paid by the Democrats for performing odd jobs, and also by the Moose Lodge for helping in the Bingo games two nights a week. Two large halls were overcrowded with people coming from as far as Milwaukee, Wisconsin to play Bingo at the Zion Moose Lodge.

At this time, my friend Mr. Rawhide advised me to apply for any job in the postal service, in order to gain experience which would be an advantage when I applied for a political job in that line of work. I did apply, and passed the necessary test. I went to work as a mail sorter in the Northbrook Post Office where, after three months, I was transferred as mailman to the Zion Post Office.

While training on the job, I had to drive a truck to make special deliveries in the mornings before going out on foot on my regular route. One day, as I drove through heavy snow, I saw a large black-and-white dog stranded in a snowbank. The snowplow that had cleared the street must have pushed the snow against him and imprisoned him where I found him. Though I had been warned by my supervisor to avoid dogs on the job, I could not help responding to the plight of an animal in distress.

I got out of my truck and into the howling snowstorm. I spoke encouraging words to the poor creature while I worked with a shovel to open a path for him to the street. When I reached him, he put his head down between his forelegs as a sign of thanks. I patted him and he rubbed his nose against me with a grateful expression in his eyes.

A few days later, as I was walking my route, a big dog came running toward me. I pulled out a can of dog repellant issued to me by the Post Office, but before I made the mistake of spraying him, I recognized the dog I'd rescued. He ran to me, uttering barks of joy and wagging his tail. He rubbed his nose on my mail bag; I spoke gently to him and patted him.

From that day on, the dog knew exactly when I'd be arriving at this spot. He would greet me there, follow me on my route, and protect me from other dogs who were vicious. He was a real character. Whenever another dog would approach me, my new friend would rush at him with a fierce growl and chase him away. Other dogs would join us on our walk, but he kept all of them at a distance so that I could move freely. The other dogs had to stay behind him; if any of them tried to move ahead of him, he chased them back.

Thus, while other mailmen were taking tetanus and anti-rabies shots and living in fear of the dogs on their routes, I enjoyed the protection of my new-found friend: my reward for a good deed.

Now, I could finally apply for a politically controlled vacancy. It was for a Rural Carrier job, not the Postmaster's I was aiming for. A Rural Carrier acts as a kind of Postmaster in the rural area. He or she sells stamps, money orders, delivers certified, registered mail, etc.; his patrons are mostly farmers and people living in rural areas. He drives his own car, which is considered a branch post office—it earns mileage allowance for him. I scored highest in a test I took with three other applicants, and Mr. Rawhide convinced the Democratic precinct captains to vote for my appointment.

I got the job. It created resentment among the old-timers who considered me an upstart. I was now a member of the National Rural Letter Carriers Association. When I asked for a refund of part of the annual dues I had paid in advance to the regular postal union, its secretary told me to forget it and consider it as a donation. He added sarcastically, "I heard you say it is a free country on several occasions. Wait 'til you feel how free it is. Your troubles have just begun."

He was the management snoop in the union who was awarded a supervisory position later on. I tried very hard to avoid trouble. I was once called on the carpet by the Postmaster, a half-educated former factory worker who, like myself, was appointed with the help of the Democrats after World War II. I was accused of insignificant mistakes (human errors). Another time, I was loading the mail into my car one snowy morning, and the Postmaster gauged my snow tires with a quarter coin; he scolded me with these words: "You better buy new tires. We do not pay you for using worn-out tires." I did not react. The Postmaster's remark about my tires was repeated by the other employees as the joke of the year.

Eventually the U.S. Postal Service was converted into a corporation, the rates went up, and the excess money was spent to convert the offices of the Post Master General in Washington, D.C., into an executive suite with new drapes, etc. The local Postmaster's office also got new drapes, carpets, air conditioners, etc. On the other hand, management went out of its way to cut the alleged sick leave abuses, changing doctor's appointments to after working hours. I once had pain in my right shoulder from bursitis, resulting from the cold draft from the car window being left open on the route for delivery of mail to patrons' boxes. I got a doctor's appointment for the next day at ten o'clock for a cortisone injection. The Postmaster called the doctor; he appealed to his civic responsibility and had him change the appointment to after working hours. I reported for work with excruciating pain. On another occasion, he denied me leave to appear in court for a case about my car being hit in the rear while driving on my route, and he changed my request to annual leave. Finally he suspended me when I applied for sick leave to go to the Mayo Clinic in Rochester, Minnesota for medical treatment of my shoulder.

Rural carriers have a union called an association. Before the last incident, Steffi contacted its president in Washington, D.C., to complain about the unjust treatment I was subjected to by the Postmaster. He replied that he could not help and suggested that I retire on disability. I did not go back to work, after I got back from the Mayo Clinic. I retired on disability based on a medical assessment issued by the Mayo Clinic. This ended my torture.

The rural carriers were a very decent bunch of people; Steffi joined its women's auxiliary. We attended many pleasant local meetings as well as state and national conventions in different parts of Illinois and the nation. I have a vivid recollection of the convention we had in San Antonio, Texas, accompanied by our granddaughter Veronica. We were carried in a large passenger boat on the river to the convention center, where the mayor and city dignitaries welcomed us with a brass band. We all had a good time, and Veronica met many youngsters of her age, children of the conventioneers. Steffi and Veronica took a side bus trip with the ladies of the convention to the Pedernales (home of President Lyndon Johnson), where they were graciously received by Lady Bird Johnson. After the convention, we visited the Alamo together, then drove to a Mexican vacation.

After high school, George went to Kendall College in Evanston. The temptation to get a job, earn money, buy his own car prevailed. He thus quit college, started working, bought a car and began enjoying a young American's life. Unfortunately it did not last very long—his car was totalled in an accident, he quarrelled with his girlfriend, and was talked into joining the army by a recruiter who promised to send him to Officers' Training School.

Once sworn in, the army sent him to a cook's school instead. At the end of his training, he was shipped to France as an army cook. In France, he was appointed supervisor in a camp for officers' dependents. He finished his studies later in life. He is now international vice president of a computer software company located in Houston, Texas. He travels all over the world visiting its customers.

After graduating from high school, Gabrielle worked in the Medical Record department of the Zion Hospital. She earned a scholarship and went to school in Lowell, Massachusetts, where she was awarded a degree of Medical Record Librarian. She joined the Victory Memorial Hospital in Waukegan, Illinois, as Assistant Medical Record Librarian. She was promoted to department head when her boss left a short time later. She is still in the same hospital in another supervisory job. She got her M.A. while she was working full time and taking care of her family. She is married to Frank Scaccia, and they have two children—Veronica and Frank Anthony. Gabrielle is an officer in the National Women in Management organization.

Joseph Sebastian (Seb) was a brilliant student. He was called the "brain" in high school. He joined the Junior Achievement organization while in high school. He was the president of his successful company which produced salad dressing, and he was awarded the title of President of the Year of the Junior Achievers at a banquet at the McCormick Convention Hall in Chicago. He has an M.A. degree in Philosophy, and is now a book publisher and publishing instructor in Berkeley, California.

Johnny (our Benjamin) did fairly well in high school, was given a small scholarship. He woke up to the challenge in Albuquerque University in New Mexico; he spent a summer in anthropological research digs in Alaska. He graduated summa cum laude in anthropology. He is married to the former Mary Doyle of Kansas City, Missouri, whom he met at the Bank of America's headquarters where both used to work. Now they live in Oakland, California. Johnny is an independent contractor in the computer science field, in which he has a degree and practical experience. John and Mary lost their lovely house in the fire that ravaged the Berkeley/Oakland Hills in 1991. They are philosophical about their material loss. Mary and John bought another house in Oakland. They will move to a new house being built on the foundation of the one that burned. They now have a son, Christopher Anthony. Our first Orfali grandson born in the good old U.S.A.

Steffi retired at age sixty-two; she joined the A.A.R.P. (American Association of Retired Persons), and was elected secretary. She also served for two years as area president. She was also appointed secretary to the city Human Relations Commission while still serving as precinct captain.

We learned quite a few things about the rights of retired people that are not publicized, in workshops offered by the A.A.R.P. in different branches we attended. We met national officers at conventions we went to. Old man Will Geer (Granpa in the Walton family serial) was the speaker in a Cincinnati convention, where I drove with a delegation of five officers of our Zion branch. We met the old gentleman at the end of the gathering and posed for pictures with him.

A short time after my retirement in September of 1977, I had to fly to Turkey to help release from detention my nephew Kevork, my brother Dick's son who lives in Italy. He had participated in anti-Turkish demonstrations in Italy and was arrested as a political agitator in Turkey, while driving through that country on his way to Iran. (Interested readers can learn more about this incident in my book *An Armenian from Jerusalem*.) In December 1977, I drove to New York City with Steffi to help celebrate the golden wedding anniversary of her cousin Gerda Dittman.

Jacob Orfali shoveling snow in Zion, Illinois

Everywhere You Go, People Are the Same

Chapter 10.

Winter in the Midwest

The 1977–78 winter was an unusually harsh one, starting with a revenge. On our way back from New York, we encountered hazardous driving with low visibility. Disabled semi-trailers in grotesque positions cluttered both sides of the highway, which resembled a continuous sheet of ice. We made it home without mishap, in time to celebrate Christmas with our children. The cold weather with below zero temperature persisted for weeks. Rain fell; it turned into ice. The tree branches and water flow from the gutters formed multicolored icicles glittering in the rays of the sun. People wore their warmest clothing indoors. The heating system worked full blast twenty-four hours a day; then as it got a bit warmer, snow began to fall. I felt lucky that I was retired and did not have to deliver mail in such weather; my heart went out to my former colleagues.

Every weekend we communicated by phone with George and his wife, who were living in Muscatine, Iowa, and Seb and Johnny who had a publishing business in Berkeley, California. We used to visit our youngest boys every year on Thanksgiving in Albuquerque, New Mexico, and celebrated it with them. We continued doing it when they moved to California. Gabrielle and her family lived in Libertyville, Illinois; either they or we called each other every day. We had the 1978 Thanksgiving meal in the brand new Marin county (California) house of our boys' friends Toni Klein and Scott Princell.

We spent the next day in Napa county, picnicking and visiting wineries. We fell in love with the area. Our boys urged us, now that we were both retired, to sell our house in Zion, move to Napa, California, and enjoy our retirement in the sunshine.

Spain: "Winter Refuge"

The 1978–79 winter in Zion was as harsh if not harsher than the 1977–78 one. We decided to take refuge in sunny Spain. We left frozen Chicago on February 11th. We landed next day in much warmer Reykjavik, capital of Iceland.

Iceland is built on volcanic rocks and has a climate of moderate heat and cold. Piped hot water from geysers supplies all the houses. We spent one night in Reykjavik, and during the day we visited indoor vegetable gardens and watched the eruption of geysers. We flew to Luxembourg the following morning and took the train to Paris. U.S travelers to Europe can buy a Euro-rail pass at reduced prices before leaving: it is good for first-class accommodations on trains all over Europe.

We called my brother Joseph from the hotel. He lives with his family in Sevres, near Paris. We visited the Louvre early in the morning and had lunch with Joseph before taking a sleeping train to Madrid, Spain. We watched as the wheels were changed to a different gauge of rails at the border. (Spain changed the gauge of its rails after it was invaded by France in the Napoleonic war. It has since reversed to the standard European gauge.)

It was not yet the tourist season. We had no trouble getting hotel accommodations in Madrid when we called from the traveler-information service at the railway station. The hotel was centrally located. We took some refreshment, then went out to explore. We ended up in the old Moorish quarter, visited the oldest church in Madrid, and had lunch in a typical Spanish restaurant recommended by our guidebook. As we entered we saw a stall of goatskins filled with wine. The food was mediocre but the wine was good and the place had interesting decorations. The guestbook was signed by famous people such as the author James A. Michener.

In the afternoon, a group of wandering minstrels in antique costumes came into the café where we were and sang old Spanish folk songs. Some ladies sitting next to our table explained to us that the performers were Spanish students who earn the money they need for their upkeep in that way.

On our second day, we boarded a ferrobus, a small commuter train, for a trip to Toledo, Spain. At the Toledo station, we took a scenic bus ride, crossed the Tajo River and ended up outside the city. We just had time to visit the Alcazar (Spanish for Al Kasr in Arabic, meaning "the castle" which may have also derived from Arabic). It was a fortress on a hill, destroyed in the Spanish civil war. It was rebuilt and is now a museum. Everything except the restaurants close in Spain for the siesta, between twelve and three. We decided to have lunch, as we were getting hungry. Francisco Franco, the Spanish dictator, had at least done one good thing for Spain: all restaurants had to offer a full meal including soup, wine and dessert (called plato de día, the day's special) for an affordable price. It was recommended by our guidebook and that is what we ordered; we were fully satisfied.

After lunch we walked through the crooked, narrow streets that led us to the cathedral. The cathedral was very impressive with its treasures of gold and silver artifacts and most impressive jewels and paintings of well-known masters. We treasured especially the unforgettable time we spent in the sacristy savoring the awe-inspiring masterpieces of El Greco. We also visited the Mudejar Santa Maria la Blanca, which was a synagogue (thirteenth and fourteenth centuries) and is now a church.

It is said that, "While in Rome, do as the Romans do!" To pass time before a late supper, the Spanish hop bars, drink wine, and consume tapas—hors d'oevres of choice dishes on small plates. We did some of what the Spanish do, we visited a bar, drank wine, and ate a few tapas; we were full and skipped dinner.

We spent most of our third morning in Spain admiring the priceless paintings of the El Prado Museum, Madrid, especially those of Goya. We bought some prints of original paintings, and took a siesta at the hotel. We visited the Royal Palace in the afternoon. The Caudillo Francisco Franco had reinstated the royalty in Spain, and the palace was again home of the Royal Family. I bought a replica of the sword of El Cid (the Lord), famous fighter from the time when Spain, shed its yoke from the Moorish occupation, and was reunited as a Christian kingdom. That evening we took the night train to Seville. We had a first-class compartment to ourselves, but could not bring ourselves to sleep. It was either too hot or too noisy because of the continuous stopping and moving. We decided not to travel any more by night in the future. We were worn out on our arrival in Seville and went right to sleep in the hotel. When we woke, we went to the cathedral, La Girondella—named the "weather cock" because of the weathervane on its tower. The tower used to be a Minaret during the Moorish occupation. We had a very good lunch at a restaurant across the street, and visited the cathedral: it was a colossal building with a dazzling altar and hand-crafted treasures of solid gold and silver. We took a ride in a horse-drawn carriage and the coachman pointed out to us some places of interest as we passed them, among them the tobacco factory in which Carmen in the Georges Bizet opera used to work.

We also went sight-seeing in the beautiful Alcazar, built on the Mudejar style by Moorish workers for their new Christian leaders. Sipping sangría in an outdoor café we relaxed; sangría, a mixture of wine and fruit juices, goes down smoothly, tastes sweet and light—it later hits you like a sledgehammer. Our evening was crowned by a rendition of flamenco dances in a famous nightclub. We enjoyed it immensely.

After our train to Cordoba and a siesta, we walked through narrow streets and peeked into picturesque courtyards of houses with attractive red tiles. The cathedral or Mesquita (mosque) is something unexpected. It is a combination of a church and mosque where Christians and Muslims prayed side by side under the same roof. The Muslim part of the building, or mosque, had low round arches of red and white stones like candy canes. At one side is the Moorish arabesque in contrast with a gothic-baroque church built next to it; the mind takes some time to get accustomed to what seems to be a confusion.

From Cordoba, the train to Algeciras was very relaxing; it passes next to green mountains, through tunnels, fruit groves, olive orchards, vineyards, etc. We boarded a ship from the harbor to Tangier in Morocco and hired a guide. He took us to a very good hotel, well beyond our budget. The next day, it was constantly raining, which restrained our activities, but we succeeded in having a glimpse of Gape Spartle and Hercules Grottoes outside the city when we visited the royal palace and its museum of Moroccan handicraft. We crossed back to Algeciras in Spain in the afternoon. Tangier was not exactly rewarding, but there are ups and downs in any journey.

We took the bus to our next stop in Malaga; the bus passes next to the Costa del Sol, "the Coast of the Sun," and the Torre Molinos ("wind mills") stretched along the Mediterranean, a much-advertised playground of the elite society. We did not like what we saw, it was nothing but an overcrowded beach surrounded by high-rises and condominiums, one next to the other; segregated housing was separated into different nationalities. At least it is good for the Spanish economy, as it brings in employment for local people and much-needed foreign currency.

When I called the hotel recommended by the Malaga travel guide, I was told it was no longer a hotel, it was now an institute to teach Spanish for foreign diplomats. The person who was speaking introduced himself as Pepe, the secretary of the institute; he offered to accommodate us in one of the free rooms. I readily accepted and we were given a pleasant room. That evening we were invited to a graduation party with all kinds of Spanish specialties, a huge dish of delicious paella, lots of wine, and music. The crowd of Norwegians, Austrians, Swiss, and Germans were the elite of their countries. The institute was on the mountain, on the way to an ancient castle.

We went downtown in the morning, visited the covered market and sampled some wine from the barrels in a retail shop. We sat in an outdoor café basking in the sun and admired a nearby beautiful fountain display and wrote postcards. We had a restful night and after a leisurely breakfast we took a bus to Nerja, called the Balcony of Europe. In Nerja, we admired the famous caves which we found to be more impressive than the Carlsbad Cavern and Mammoth Caves in the United States. We had a delightful lunch on the terrace with a view over mountains and sea on the Balcony of Europe.

Our train ride to Granada seemed endless; the train seemed to meander around mountains all over Spain. There was only one track, so we had to stop to let incoming trains pass. We booked into the only hotel that was not closed for winter. We saw the famous Alhambra, most celebrated of all the monuments left by the Moors, with part of the original Sierra Nevada in the background. Next to Alhambra are the buildings the Generalife and Torres Bermejas. It would take a whole chapter to write about the wonders found in the Alhambra.

The name Alhambra means "the red" in Arabic. It derives from the red bricks of which the outer walls are built. The Torres Bermejas means the "Crimson Towers" in Spanish. Many books have been written in English about the exquisite buildings and gardens of the Alhambra; the Alhambra by Washington Irving is a collection of stories from Moorish times.

The cathedral of Granada contains many paintings and sculptures by Alonso Cano. In one of its numerous chapels, one known as Capilla Real—Royal Chapel—is the tomb of Ferdinand and Isabella, first rulers of united Spain.

When we went back to the hotel, we were exhausted from the cold weather and the snow had started to fall. We drank a whole bottle of strong red Spanish wine to warm up and went to bed dizzy.

In Valencia, our next stop, our hotel was not one of the best. The restaurant recommended by the hotel did not serve paella, which originated in Valencia. We will have paella in Valencia on our next visit to that city.

We had a delightful short train ride to Barcelona. Along the sea, the train was very comfortable and we were served a delicious meal at our seats.

The hotel recommended by the guidebook in Barcelona was

very good, and in the center of the town. After we made first-class train reservations for Switzerland, we had sangría with Spanish seafood in a bar next to the hotel in a relaxed atmosphere. We stayed only one day in Barcelona and went to the Pueblo Español in the morning. It is a large compound, with streets and buildings representing the different styles of the provinces of Spain. I bought a replica of Columbus's ship, Santa Maria, and an original painting of a Spanish street by a well-known modern Spanish painter. After a short siesta, we took a tour to the Tibidabo mountain, the unfinished church of the Sacred Family (Sacrada Familia) by Gaudi, and the museum housing the early work of Picasso. We enjoyed visiting again the strangely wonderful cathedral which we had seen on a previous trip. By then it was getting late, so we had a nightcap and went to bed.

The "Catalan" that we took next morning was one of the best trains in Europe, and offered utter comfort. We intended to stop and spend the night in picturesque Avignon, France, but were engrossed in an epicurean gourmet dinner in the dining car and decided to carry on to Geneva, Switzerland. We could not get much for our United States dollars in Geneva. We spent the night and left early next day for Munich, Germany, a town we like very much and keep returning to.

As soon as we got settled in the hotel, we went to Hofbrau, the famous beergarten, where we drank beer, enjoyed very good food, listened to oompha-oompha music, and joined the crowd in singing German folk songs. The Bavarians seem to be gifted in finding ways to enjoy whatever is available to them, regardless of their financial situation.

Next day we went to Garmisch Partenkirchen and took the Zugspitzenbahn, a cogwheel train that climbs to the summit of the highest mountain in Germany. On top of the mountain, one side is German territory and the other side is Austrian. I walked to the Austrian side and came to a deserted building, the frontier control post.

In Munich I had an Agfa camera repaired, bought woolen blankets (Steppdecken), and we found time for a short visit to the

Frauenkirche (the nuns' church).

We took the train for the last time to Luxembourg and boarded our plane back home. The cold weather in the midwest had subsided in the meantime.

AUXILIARY CATECHIST

This diploma is awarded by the Christian Brothers

to _____JACOB G. ORFALI_____

in recognition of successful completion of the

TEACHER TRAINING COURSE IN CHRISTIAN DOCTRINE

at _____St. Joseph Parish_____Waukegan_____

Date_____May 9, 1962_____

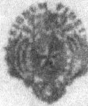

Brother Albert
Teacher of Course

Brother H. Albert
Chairman, Archdiocese of Chicago

Brother J. Philip
Provincial of the Christian Brothers

The

Confraternity of ⛨ Christian Doctrine
Archdiocese of Chicago

This is to certify that

MR. JACOB G. ORFALI

has successfully completed the prescribed Confraternity Teacher-Training Course in

METHODS

Given under our hand and seal this 25th day of May
in the year of Our Lord 19 62

+ Albert Cardinal Meyer
ARCHBISHOP OF CHICAGO

Laurence W. Ryan
DIRECTOR

The Christian Brothers certificate s earned by Jacob Orfali in 1962. Above, for completion of the Teacher Training course in Christian Doctrine. Below , for the Teacher Training Course in Methods, awarded by Cardinal Albert Meyer, then head of the Catholic Archdiocese of Chicago

Jacob Orfali

Stephanie Orfali during the winter of 1978 in Zion, Illinois

Everywhere You Go, People Are the Same

Chapter 11.

Our Last Winter in the Midwest
and Move to California

The Arctic cold hit the midwest again before the Spring of 1979. We were faced with several feet of snow as we got up one morning, and more was falling.

I could not keep up with shovelling the snow. After cleaning the walk on one side of the house, I moved to the other side; as soon as I cleared this side and went back to the first one to get into the house, it was covered by one foot of snow. I gave up the losing battle and decided to call professional help after the snow stopped falling. Some snow stuck to the outside of the window on the landing facing our bedroom and turned into ice. It melted when exposed to the rays of the sun and somehow it penetrated inside the window. We were thus faced with a leak in the window for the first time after fifteen years of living in that house.

We now considered selling our house and moving to a warmer climate. We hired professionals to repair the leak in the window and give the house a new paint job as soon as the weather permitted.

We then asked a friend in the real estate business to appraise the house for us. We were not happy with his appraisal figure, and we decided to sell the house without an agent. We advertised in the paper—we had to put up with the usual hustlers whose only interest, we felt, was to give us a hard time.

No serious buyers were at hand. We became resigned to spending another winter in the house and try again to sell next spring. A day after the ad appeared for the last time, a couple living ten minutes' drive from our house made an appointment to come and see it that afternoon.

The house had two independent rental units in addition to the section of our two-bedroom apartment; it also had a basement that I used as workshop where I made my wine. The interested party came accompanied by the husband's old father. The old man saw my two five-gallon jars with cherry juice from the garden cherry trees, in the process of being made into wine. I explained to him in detail how I make cherry and other wines, which impressed them all very much. I offered them some of the previous year's cherry wine while discussing the deal.

During our discussion, I leaned that the husband worked as a boiler inspector for a company, and his wife was a CPA working from an office in their home at Wadsworth. They were buying the house as an investment: there was always a demand for rental apartments, by the personnel of the Great Lakes Naval Station, a thirty-minute drive from the house. We closed the deal with $20,000 more than the amount suggested by our friend, the real-estate broker.

Movers were to come and pack the things to be moved to California, our destination. It would be kept stored until we rented a house there. We sold or gave away what was left over. Our daughter Gabrielle helped Steffi in the final cleaning of the house. Seb had also come from California to help us pack and discard whatever he did not need from his stuff that was kept in the attic. We were ready when the new owners showed up—we handed over the keys and gave them a five-gallon container full of brewing cherry juice.

A second similar container was loaded in the station wagon to take with us to California. The constant shaking of the travel made it the best wine I had ever made. Seb drove his mother (Steffi) to the Illinois State Park for a last look at Lake Michigan. Gabrielle drove her car and I drove my station wagon.

We were all to meet in Libertyville at the Scaccia home (Gabrielle's married name) and spend the night with the family.

Leaving Illinois

We left early the next morning, Saturday, August 11, 1979, in our two cars; in addition to the brewing wine, they contained some of our personal belongings and clothing, to hold us over until we got settled in our future home. Gabrielle drove Steffi's eight-cylinder Dodge Dart and I drove our Dodge Colt station wagon. Gabrielle's son Frank Anthony came along. He and Steffi alternated as passengers in one car or the other. We had decided to make a picnic of our travel and enjoy the scenery. We stopped at Battleship Rock in Wisconsin, then in Dresbach, Minnesota, where we picnicked and drove through Minnesota as far as Austin, where we spent the night.

Just before reaching the Bad Lands, South Dakota, we stopped at a motel with a swimming pool, to the special delight of our grandson Frank.

We rose early the next day and were driving in the Bad Lands by eight a.m., where we breakfasted in a pleasant lodge. We drove leisurely through the fascinating moon landscape of the Bad Lands, stopping to enjoy views and take pictures. We visited a gold mine in Keystone and were given a hammer and chisel to cut a piece of rock ore for a souvenir (it may or may not contain traces of gold). We walked among the souvenir shops and watched a slide show about the famous Mount Rushmore. The scenery around Keystone is breathtaking; Mount Rushmore is worth seeing. Frank was especially excited about the enormous heads of the presidents cut in the rock. We took pictures from every vantage point and watched men doing some work on the heads: they looked as tiny as flies!

Our next stop was at the Crazy Horse monument, a short distance from Mount Rushmore. Here, an old Pole (originally from Poland) with his family are busy carving a monument in a mountain, of the Indian Chief Crazy Horse mounted on his beautiful steed. The outlines of the monument can already be distinguished. It will take many years to finish the superhuman task. We spent the night in a beautiful Best Western Motel, but it was too cold to enjoy their tempting outdoor pool.

On Tuesday, we left for Custer through forests and mountain roads to Buffalo. We then drove high up to Powder River Pass. We drove slowly to enjoy the scenery. Through Ten Sleep, we pushed on to Warlance and stayed again at a Best Western Motel.

On Wednesday, we reached the zenith of our trip, and more than halfway on our trek. The ascent to Yellowstone National Park is thrilling. In all our travels, we had not encountered anything as spectacular as Yellowstone Park. At the lodge near Lake Yellowstone we got a "Luxury Cabin."

A splendid view of a lovely lake was a foretaste of what to expect. At the interesting boiling mud volcanoes, we walked for miles with a little guidebook and we were intrigued by the boiling mud puddles and the smell of sulphur they emitted. We then drove to the waterfalls and awe-inspiring Grand Canyon of Yellowstone. We walked 'til our feet could no longer carry us, taking pictures left and right.

Our cabin had four beds and a round table with chairs where we ate a cold supper. We watched an interesting slide show given by an old sympathetic ranger who narrated the slides. They were about winter in Yellowstone Park. The narrative included lots of personal experiences and his answers to questions left no doubt that he was in love with his job.

The next day we took off to Old Faithful. We drove some slow thirty· miles from the lake through deep forest: we saw many herds of animals such as American Bison, mountain sheep, antelope, etc., in clearings. When we reached Old Faithful, it obliged us with an eruption. We watched a movie about geysers, then saw another geyser that erupts once a day—it honoured us with a beautiful performance.

We continued our tour through geyser country following footmarked paths. Other than geysers, each with a different personality and pattern of eruption, there were hot water pools and springs. They all had colorful descriptive names. On our way back to the restrooms next to Old Faithful, it shot out again with an even more powerful eruption than before.

Friday: this day we covered many miles and enjoyed scenery

of unbelievable beauty. We had the Great Tetons for companions for a long stretch over passes and canyons. It was so much to absorb all at once that we felt kind of dizzy. We only hoped that the photos we had taken would succeed in giving full credit to the dazzling beauty of nature as we had seen it. At Ogden, Utah, we stayed for the night after a fine dinner at the Sizzler.

We arrived early in Salt Lake City after a lengthy breakfast served by the slowest waitress in the U.S.A. We joined a conducted tour of the Temple and learned about the Church of Jesus Christ of Latter Day Saints. Their story seems very far-fetched, but they seemed sincere and a good bunch of people. We stopped at the Great Salt Lake, where we wanted to swim, but the water was so shallow that we could only wade in the lake. With overcast sky, it was reasonably cool and this made it easy to cross the Great Salt Lake Desert.

We, of course, had to stop at the first occasion we had in Nevada for a fling at the one-armed bandits. At Elko we stayed overnight and enjoyed gambling, resulting in a moderate loss.

By Reno, we had most of the driving behind us. We swam in our motel pool, and went to the Circus-Circus Casino, where children are welcome at the midway games and where grandson Frank spent money liberally, having a great time. We had a good buffet lunch at Circus-Circus. In the evening Frank had to stay in the motel watching TV; we three grown-ups went to a show at Harold's: a musical revue named "the Bordello." It was a bawdy, funny show. Gabrielle remarked, "That is not exactly a show to go to with your parents." After the show, we again tried our luck gambling.

Monday morning, we had breakfast at Circus-Circus, but avoided gambling. The ladies felt their small loss was worth the fun they had. I don't like to waste my time with the machines; I had played seven-card stud (poker). I left Reno with more money than I came with.

We enjoyed the wonderful descending drive on Highway 80, and arrived in Berkeley, California, where our sons Seb and John live, about noontime. We went straight to Seb's house where it was arranged by phone that we would meet. Seb offered us the use of a little room in his garden, while looking for a house to buy. Gabrielle and Frank stayed in the small apartment of John's girlfriend. We did not mind sleeping on just mattresses on the carpeted floor, it felt like being on a camp-out. The weather was perfect.

We spent the first few days sight-seeing with Gabrielle and Frank. We went to Muir Woods, Golden Gate Park, had tea in the Japanese Tea Garden of Golden Gate Park—we even took time to watch a baseball game in Candlestick Park. Unluckily for us from Illinois, the Giants beat the Cubs.

We looked for houses in Walnut Creek, Sebastopol, Calistoga and Napa. We found the ideal house in our preferred city of Napa. It has three bedrooms, a living room, a family room, a kitchen, a dining room, two washrooms (one with a bathtub and the second with a shower next to the master bedroom). Plus a covered patio, a large flowerbed, and an enclosed vegetable and fruit garden. We also had a Jacuzzi installed.

Though the house cost almost double what we got for the house in Zion, it was a good buy for California. In the meantime, its value has appreciated to more than double what it cost. At that time, we received a phone call from my brothers that my mother passed away in the hospital, where she was treated for different old-age sicknesses. Soon after we closed the deal on the house, I left on Labor Day for Amman, Jordan where my mother lived with my youngest sister Nelly and my brothers.

In Amman, I attended the official funeral services and paid my respects at my mother's grave. There was a large reception after the Funeral Mass at the house of my brothers, with a catered lunch. It was attended by a substantial number of relatives and friends.

We moved to our new house in the lovely Napa Valley in late September. We are very happy with our decision to relocate to California. We thank the gods who led us to this valley and our lovely house. With the passage of time, we made new acquaintances, acquiring friends at the Autobiography course we attended at the Napa Valley College to improve our writing skill. We joined a Bowling League for Seniors of which I was later elected president for two consecutive years. I also served as vice-president for two years in the Home Owners Association of our area. Steffi transferred her membership of the League of Women Voters from Zion to Napa, and has served as officer in functions other than that of president. The presidency was offered to her several times, but she refused to take it.

I took a course in making Ming trees given by a Filipino teacher who learned it in the Orient; it complements the jewelry-making courses I attended in Illinois when I retired. I am manager in charge of Printed Supplies for the whole SIRS (Sons in Retirement) organization of California. I procure all the printed forms required for the efficient running of the organization. The stock of supplies is stored in my garage. It is shipped to the assistant manager when ordered. I head eight assistant managers in different parts of California; each one of them supplies printed matter to between 22 and 25 branches of his area. I was appointed to an additional duty of "Chairman of Forms Committee." Together with my committee, we will revise all forms, we will recommend to the president of the SIRS the elimination of obsolete forms and have new forms printed, as and when required.

All the above activities, in addition to the time I spend taking care of the garden and small repairs of our home appliances, ought to keep me out of trouble. We drive very often to San Francisco to meet friends; we used to go regularly to the San Francisco Opera, but had to cancel our subscription to avoid excessive driving. We still go to the excellent concerts performed by the very gifted Napa Valley Symphony.

We are constantly in touch with our two youngest boys (Seb and John) and their mates, who either visit us or we visit them. We take every occasion to get together for dinners, birthdays, and other functions. Our other children and families are happy for every excuse they can use to come for a family visit. Most of our relatives and friends from France, Italy, Jordan and Israel, etc., as well as the different states of the Union, have visited us and stayed in our Napa home. We enjoy having a house full of guests, for outdoor shishkebab, Thanksgiving dinners, Christmas, and New Year's celebrations.

We, of course, have our share of old age (unavoidable) "aches and pains," which we try not to let slow us too much. That, in a "big nutshell," is the state of our present life.

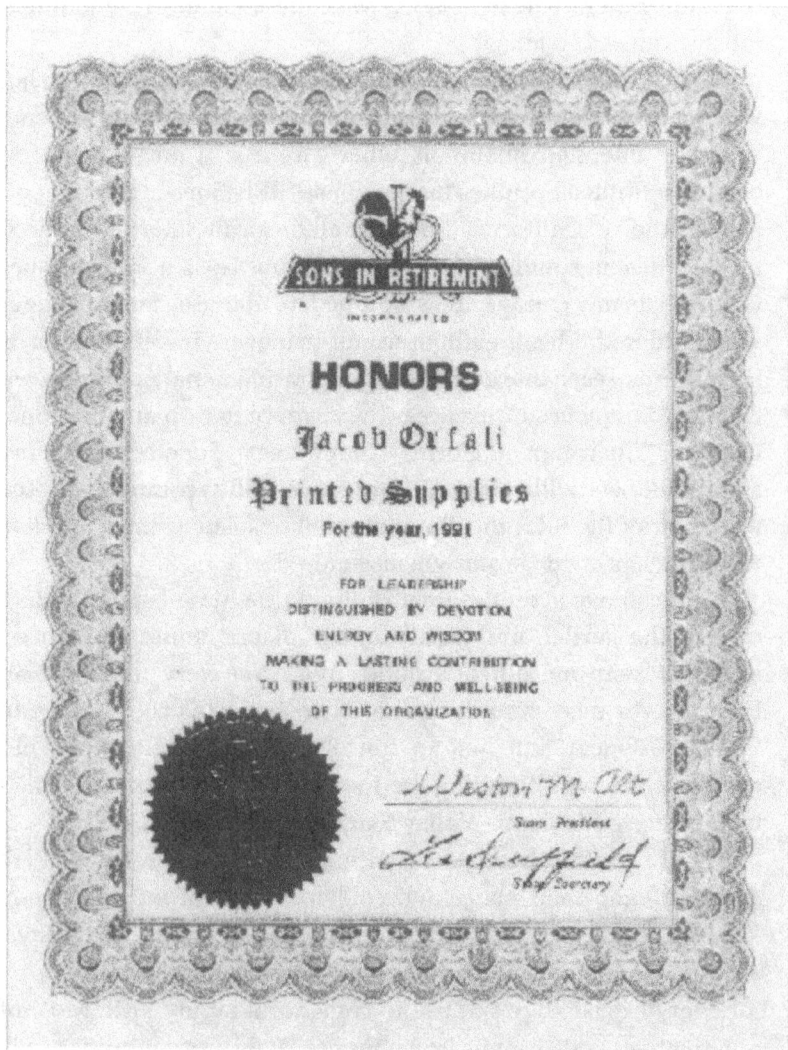

*Certificate awarded to Jacob Orfali by the SIRS (Seniors in Retirement)
for his service to the organization*

Everywhere You Go, People Are the Same

Christopher Orfali, the first Orfali born in the USA

*Celebrating the 85th birthday of "Oma" (grandmother) Braun,
the mother of Stephanie Orfali*

Everywhere You Go, People Are the Same

Chapter 12.

A Hectic Trip

Three months after the Six-Day War in the Holy Land (Israel), in mid-September 1967, I traveled to that unfortunate country. I arranged to see family members near Paris and in Rome on the way.

The Air France plane I boarded in Chicago stopped at Montreal, Quebec, and a Quebequois or French Canadian who took the seat next to mine was pleased when I greeted him in French. He had married a local girl while serving in France during World War II, he said, and she was visiting her folks. He was on his way to meet them. The hostesses served a delicious French meal which we washed down with Bordeaux wine over the Atlantic Ocean. After the movie, we settled down to sleep in our seats.

At dawn the hostesses opened the curtains and the Captain let us know that we were on schedule and would land at Paris in an hour. Although the sky was foggy he anticipated no problem. After breakfast when the seat belt light came on, we prepared for landing. We then heard the Captain's voice: he had not yet gotten permission to land, on account of heavy fog with zero visibility, but said he had fuel for another hour and would continue to circle over Paris, waiting for clearance. If necessary, he could land at Le Bourget in downtown Paris.

We all looked at our watches, getting uneasy as the end of the hour of grace got nearer with no new announcement from the Captain. At this time a deep silence pervaded the plane, broken only by the faint click-click of the rosaries that some older passengers were using in their prayers for help; it sounded like an urgent S.O.S. or May Day distress signal. Even the baby who had cried during the night respected this conspiracy of silence.

My Canadian neighbor nudged me and whispered, "What do you think?" I answered nonchalantly, "Don't worry; we will make it," maybe more to reassure myself than him. A few minutes later the Captain announced that he was proceeding to the champagne country to land in a military airport near Rheims. I got the feeling that the rosary beads click-clicked more urgently at this time to compensate for the fuel shortage which the Captain failed to mention.

When we finally landed at Rheims, we were not allowed to leave the plane and walk around in the military restricted zone. We waited in the stuffy plane with the air conditioning turned off for the security people to clear us, with no drinking water. After an hour of this we were herded to the office, where our passports were stamped.

The customs officers were said to be on their way. After we tired of waiting for them, I went to see the security chief with a delegation of passengers. I told him that we had given preference to Air France over other airlines and came as guests to spend our money in France; we were all tired and hungry and surely deserved better treatment. He replied, "Please give me a few minutes to confer with my helpers." A heated discussion followed, with Gallic temper intermingled with shouts and laughter; at the end they decided to let us leave the airport without opening our luggage.

With no time to visit the famous Cathedral of Rheims, I joined the other passengers in a special train to Paris. On the way we ate very fine sandwiches of pate de fois gras, mortadella sausages, cold roast beef, cheeses, wine, beer, and fruit. At the Paris station we were welcomed with new reservations by Air France agents. They took us in cabs to the airport, where they gave us credit vouchers for dinner in the best restaurant and wished us Bon Voyage. I called my local brother since there was no time to visit him now.

After strolling in the airport shopping area, by the time I reached the restaurant I had a good appetite. I noticed that a waiter was having a communication problem with an old lady. From the way she was dressed, she seemed to be from Eastern Europe; she must have been a transit passenger on her way to the Western Hemisphere. A second waiter who seemed to know some Slavic languages joined them. I heard him say "sopa", and after a while she was served a large bowl of lentil soup with a pile of bread.

Then my waiter brought me a plate of cold cuts and bread. Though I was hungry I did not touch the food but kept discreetly watching the old lady's table. They gave her an orange when she finished the soup and she left after eating it. This hit a raw nerve in me. She was served a cheap meal, whereas the restaurant would be paid for a good, full dinner. I beckoned the waiter to my table and asked him, "Is this my dinner?" When he said, "Yes, Sir," I called for the head waiter, who came smiling and inquired, "What can I do for you, Sir?" I said, "I am entitled to a French dinner and I intend to get it. If this is the new fashion in French cuisine, I prefer the old way, with soup, entrée, salad, wine, dessert, cheese, and coffee," and I added with a raised voice, "Do I look to you like a person coming from Eastern Europe, like the poor old lady who was seated at the next table?" At this, the head waiter begged me to keep my voice down. He said that there must have been a mistake, for which he apologized, and he would personally see that I got complete satisfaction. He succeeded; the food was exquisite, the wine a poem to the palate, and the service impeccable. After coffee, I smoked an Habana cigar and sipped Benedictine liqueur.

At the hotel in Rome, the clerk proposed to another young man and myself: "You two, Mr. Orfali and Mr. Mazzoni, are Italian. I cannot charge you the same as others, so I propose that you share a large room with two big, comfortable separate beds and a private bathroom together, at half the price of what I charge others." We readily accepted. My roommate was a very nice person of Italian ancestry, from New York.

The next morning I took a quick tour of the Villa Borguese, the Pantheon with the open ceiling and the storm drains in the floor.

This building, originally a Roman temple, is now used as a Christian church. We also visited the Vatican, and St. Peter's Basilica and Square.

After an overnight in Beirut, Lebanon, because no planes were allowed to fly over Jordan after dark for security reasons, I flew into Amman. I spent a week with my family and visited Petra, the famous Nabathean city on the ancient caravan route linking Egypt to the Far East. I also went to Jerash, of Roman, Greek, and Crusaders' fame.

No one was allowed to cross the Allenby Bridge over the Jordan River from Jordan into Israel after the West Bank was occupied by Israeli forces during the Six-Day War. In order to reach Jerusalem, instead of taking the road over the bridge, which would have taken ninety minutes, I had to fly to Cypress and from there to Ben Gurion Airport.

I stayed at my mother-in-law's house in the new city of Jerusalem and visited the scenes of recent fighting that extended from the old city of Jerusalem to the Jordan River. Skeletons of tanks destroyed by napalm bombs were all over the highway. I was speechless at the sight of burnt-out personnel carriers, all around the Inn of the Good Samaritan on the way to Jericho. It reminded me of Dante's inferno. All of this in the land of the patriarchs, the prophets, and the saints, venerated by the world's three major religions of Judaism, Christianity, and Islam! They all preach love and brotherhood, but cannot practice what they preach.

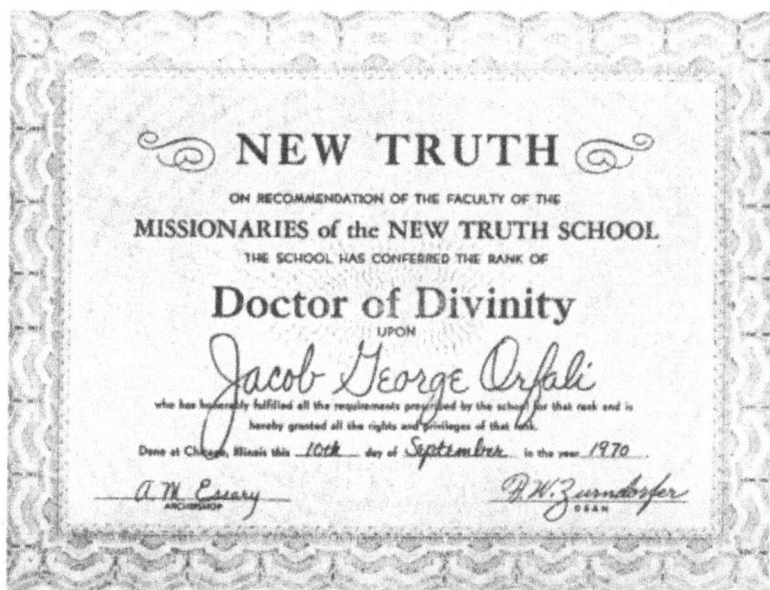

The "Doctor of Divinity" diploma received from the New Truth School by Jacob Orfali in 1970

Jacob Orfali in Malaga, Spain

Everywhere You Go, People Are the Same

Chapter 13.

1981 Spring Vacation in Egypt

In the fall of 1980 we decided to take our spring vacation in the Middle East. We planned our tour with Ken and Alice Smetts, then wrote to Mr. Kanstedt, our travel agent in Illinois. Kanstedt was a Swede who had served us very well when we lived in Zion, Illinois. He was dedicated to his work, and planned the most efficient travel arrangements at the lowest cost.

My wife Steffi wanted to spend a few days with our son George and his wife Judy in Muscatine, Iowa, and with our daughter Gaby and her family in Libertyville, Illinois. On the morning of April 11 I drove her to the San Francisco Airport and she flew to Moline, Illinois. George and Judy picked her up and drove her to their home in Muscatine. The next day they drove to meet our daughter's family in Libertyville and enjoyed a family reunion. Gaby took off from work on the 13th and 14th to accompany Steffi on visits to old friends in Zion and Waukegan, Illinois.

On April 13, after a hectic day of preparations, I spent the night at the Smetts's home in Lafayette. The next day an uncle of theirs drove the three of us to San Francisco Airport, where we took a TWA flight to Chicago. Steffi, Gaby, her husband Luis, and our grandson Frank met us there. After checking in our baggage for the overseas flight, we had a fond visit with them in the cocktail lounge.

We boarded a KLM plane at 4 P.M. We watched a movie after dinner, then took a nap. After a smooth and uneventful flight, we landed in Amsterdam, Holland, the next morning at 8:15 local time. We had four hours to kill before our flight to Egypt began, and the Smettses would have liked to see Amsterdam, but we were told there might not be enough time. The mall at Amsterdam Airport is a shopper's dream, however, and while I took a rest on a convenient sofa, Steffi, Ken, and Alice toured the shops.

At 12:15 our plane took off for Cairo. We made a one-hour stopover at Istanbul Airport in Turkey. This airport had been controlled by the military since the overthrow of the civilian government. Only the passengers whose final destination was Istanbul were allowed to leave the plane. We watched uncomfortably as the soldiers frisked them. At the end of the hour, we flew off again, to reach Cairo at 6 P.M. It was rainy and sticky and hot. The immigration officials stamped our passports without questioning us. A security officer eyed Ken's hand luggage, which bulged with a variety of cameras, lenses, and other photography equipment. For security reasons, no photographs may be taken of the airport, but the officer performed a perfunctory inspection and waved Ken on.

Soon we spotted a well-dressed man who carried a sign reading: "Mr. and Mrs. Orfali and Smetts, the Peace Agency welcomes you to Cairo." He introduced himself as our travel agent. He helped us through customs, where our luggage was not inspected, then led us through a wire fence. A crowd of people wearing nightshirts, "*gallabiahs*, national attire of Egyptian males," gaped at us as we came out, and I wondered whether we looked as strange to them as they looked to us.

When we were seated in the travel agency's minibus, their representative outlined to us the schedule of our visit to Egypt and gave us a copy of it. He accompanied us to the Hyatt Prince Hotel in Nasser City, checked us in, and told us to be ready at eight the next morning for the first step of our tour. We had expected to spend a day relaxing and recovering from jet lag, but we accepted the plan.

When we settled in our hotel room, we discovered other discrepancies between the schedule given us by the agent and the one we'd received from our travel agent in the States. We called the Smettses and visited their room to discuss these changes. When we got there, Alice said, "Do you know what I'm going to do as soon as you leave?"

"I know," said Steffi, "I saw those complimentary packs of bubble bath. I'm going to use them as soon as I get back to our room."

I was tense from the long flight and asked Ken to join me in a walk. He accepted readily, because he wanted to change some money into Egyptian currency and buy drinking water. Visitors to Egypt are advised not to use tap water for drinking or even for brushing their teeth. Plastic bottles of Evian water, imported from France, are sold in every shop. On all our excursions over the next few days, we passed tourists of both sexes and all ages hugging their precious bottles of Evian water.

Outside the hotel, we had our first face-to-face encounter with the natives. They were very friendly. Passersby directed us through dark alleys to get to the shops, but nobody bothered us. My knowledge of Arabic was helpful, of course.

Steffi was asleep when I returned, but awakened as I opened the door. I asked if she'd enjoyed her bubble bath. She replied that she'd been too exhausted to take it yet, but would do so now. I was still too wound up to sleep, so I began to write out my notes on our travels up to this point. When Steffi finished her bath, I took one too, and finally found myself able to sleep.

On April 16, our real adventure in Egypt began. I jumped out of bed at 6 A.M., full of curiosity and expectations, and went for a morning walk. At the entrance to the hotel I saw a line of buses, surrounded by tourists speaking French, German, Spanish, and English, all waiting to depart. Government offices for different departments were near our hotel. People clustered around handcarts—"portable restaurants," as they were called—buying the traditional Egyptian breakfast: a couple of spoonfuls of overcooked fava beans topped with raw olive oil, shatta (a hot pepper sauce), and raw onions, scooped up with flat bread, and washed down with cold water. I was again amazed at the open friendliness of the people who, when I greeted them in Arabic, invited me to share their meager meal.

I got back to the hotel in time to eat an American-style buffet breakfast with lots of goodies, both Western and oriental: fresh fruits, coffee, tea, and the inevitable cereals. The excursion minibus arrived, and the agent introduced us to our guide, a nice-looking, slender Coptic girl. She announced that today we would visit Memphis and Sakkara, and stop for lunch in a restaurant near the Great Pyramid.

On our way, we stopped downtown to pick up another American couple at the Shepherd Hotel. At this point we got our first sight of the real Cairo, a city of over ten million people: overpopulated, polluted, swarming with chaotic traffic. Filth and garbage were piled in the streets to rot in the heat. We noticed many unfinished houses; laundry was hung from their windows, showing that they were inhabited. The guide explained that most of the skilled laborers preferred to leave Egypt to work in the oil-rich Arab countries, where they could earn in one month what they could not earn in a year at home. This was the reason for most of the disorganization and the many unfinished construction jobs. The continuous influx of landless people from the rural areas, combined with the lack of adequate housing, created a serious problem. Squatters had even invaded the impressive family mausoleums of the wealthy in the cemeteries, converting them to living quarters.

Once we got out into the country, we were in an entirely different world. We couldn't help admiring the well-disciplined activities of the fellahin, or farmers. They were as busy as bees, transforming every drop of the Nile River into fertile green fields. They looked clean, well-fed, and handsome in their *gallabiahs* (elegant robes). We watched the Nile flow proudly through this lovely scene. We saw herds of gamus, or water buffalo, moving languidly on the shore, and passed donkey-drawn carts piled with produce as we moved on toward Memphis.

In Memphis, we were fascinated by the ruins of the temples, the unique Alabaster Sphinx of Ramses II, and the colossal and beautiful statue of Ramses II. This statue is carved from a single gigantic block of hard crystalline limestone, which resembles marble. When standing, it had risen to a height of 44 feet, but its feet are now missing and it lies on its back. The face certainly is that of a handsome man. Next to the ruins stands a well-kept grove of date palms.

From Memphis, we drove to Sakkara. We stopped at a carpet workshop on the way, to watch in amazement as the deft fingers of a youngster moved over a primitive loom, weaving a carpet on which he recreated from memory scenes from the walls of the ancient tombs.

At Sakkara we visited the Step Pyramids Complex, which contains the oldest stone buildings in the world. Kings and other noble and famous people were buried here in *mastabahs* (tombs with sloping sides and flat roofs). The Pyramid of King Unas, of the Fifth Dynasty, is worthy of special attention. After crawling into the burial chambers, we admired the inner walls, which were completely covered with the earliest uninterrupted hieroglyphic writing covering such a huge area. It represents the secret formula discovered by Unas, which would convey his soul over the celestial path to be united with the Solar System and become part of it.

On our way to the Great Pyramid, after a well-prepared lunch, we crept 128 feet, stooping over all the way, to the burial chambers at the top of the Great Pyramid. Later we visited all the other pyramids in the complex, and the Great Sphinx, most famous of all the sphinxes. Our day ended at the papyrus-making workshop, where we were shown the different stages in the process for making papyrus, and viewed an exhibition of hand paintings on papyrus, which were for sale. This was our last stop of the day; when we reached the hotel we were too tired to undertake any further explorations.

On April 17, we toured the city of Cairo. We started at a citadel built by Saladin, partly from stones borrowed from the Great Pyramid Complex. Then we visited the Mohammad Ali Alabaster Mosque, where we were shown the famous clock exchanged for the obelisk that now stands in Paris. By the way, the clock never

Jacob Orfali   119

worked properly, or showed the correct time. It is resting now, as mere decoration.

We then visited the Sultan Hassan Mosque. It's forbidden to enter a mosque with your street shoes on; in the old days they had to be removed and left outside. Modern times have caught up with this custom: now they slip shoe-shaped cloths over your shoes and charge you for them. We also saw the mosque where the late Shah of Iran is buried. It's protected by a 24-hour watch, to protect it from desecration, and the public is not allowed near it.

Next we visited the renowned Egyptian Museum, which houses the most magnificent treasures of the ancient Pharaohs. Unfortunately, it was Friday, so the museum closes from 12 to 2 P.M. for prayers. We managed only a quick walk through the most famous exhibits before we were escorted out at noon.

We were taken to the world-famous Khan Khalili Bazaars, which were crowded with men wearing *gallabiahs* and with veiled women. The streets were bordered by curio shops that overflowed with leather goods, expensive jewelry, copperware, and other handmade items. It reminded us of a scene from the Arabian tales of the *Thousand and One Nights*.

Next we visited the Coptic Church of the Holy Family. In its basement is a room where, according to tradition, the Holy Family stayed after their flight from Bethlehem. We were then led to the Synagogue of Ben Ezra. This rickety building is unsafe to enter and is being rehabilitated, but the old rabbi in residence there showed us a dirty-looking body of water, which he told us was the cleansing pool where the faithful submerged themselves before prayer. It was, he told us, a branch of the Nile where the basket containing the infant Moses was found by the Pharaoh's daughter, who adopted him.

As we moved around Cairo, we encountered donkey-drawn garbage carts, shabby-looking vehicles hauling a stinking load. The city does not pay for garbage collection; on the contrary, the job is contracted to the highest bidders, who sell the garbage to the farmers as fertilizer. We also saw the famous overcrowded streetcars of Cairo, with their passengers sitting on the roof and hanging onto the doors and windows.

That night we had a sumptuous feast in the elaborate hotel restaurant: uniformed waiters served us stuffed pigeons and we washed these down with Ptolemy wine, grown by Greeks in the Sinai desert.

The next day, we woke up at 4:30 A.M. We were driven to the airport to catch the 6:30 plane to Aswan, via Luxor. It was a very comfortable French-built "Air Bus." Our fellow passengers were from many countries, and we could hear German, French, Spanish, English, and Hebrew being spoken around us.

We had a strange experience upon reaching Aswan: we were treated to music from the Yiddish musical comedy *Fiddler on the Roof* aboard an Egyptian Misr Air flight.

We were met at the airport by the agent, a handsome young Nubian, and were taken to the Hotel Cataract in a car driven by another Nubian. We later found out that a large number of Nubians live in Aswan. They have their own language and customs, and there is even a nightclub where Nubian dances are performed. They live in a village of their own. They had to leave their homeland when their lands were flooded and Lake Nasser was created upon completion of the High Dam.

At our hotel we were introduced to our guide, another young Nubian man with an infectious sense of humor. He was a good guide and a fine entertainer. His great ambition was to emigrate to America and make his fortune.

We were taken in *falucas* (sailboats) in the first cataract of the Nile to visit Kitchener's Botanic Island, which contains a beautiful garden of tropical plants, some of which were brought from India by Lord Kitchener. We saw the mausoleum erected on the Western bank of the Nile in memory of the Aga Khan, leader of the Ismaeli Muslims. We also visited the Elephantine Island, which resembles a group of bathing elephants, the ruins of the temple of the ram-headed god Khnum, and an early Christian church. We also saw a "Nilometer," which measured the height of the water. The tax collectors in ancient times used it to determine how much tax should be levied on the crops of the land irrigated by the Nile.

In the afternoon, after lunch at the hotel, we went to see the new High Dam (*Sadd el Aali* in Arabic), seven miles from the old Aswan Dam. The Aswan Dam was constructed as a cooperative venture by Egypt and Great Britain between 1898 and 1902; at that time it was the largest dam in the world.

On the way to the High Dam, we stopped at the granite quarries, the source of the red and gray granite used to build the ancient Egyptian monuments. Here we saw an unfinished obelisk, 92 feet high and 10.6 feet wide. It had apparently been rejected when a flaw, which we were able to see, was detected in it.

The ancient Egyptians took clever advantage of Mother Nature's assistance. To quarry granite, they simply drilled holes in the rock around the piece they needed, inserted sticks of wood into the holes, and poured water around the sticks. The resulting expansion of the wood broke off a neatly cut block of granite. These blocks were conveyed to the construction site by barges on the Nile.

The High Dam is a true marvel. Besides generating electricity, it was designed to irrigate enough land to nourish all of Egypt. Unfortunately, the high birth rate of the Egyptians makes this task increasingly difficult. The Russians, who helped build the dam, erected a lotus-shaped monument there to commemorate Russo-Egyptian friendship. Our guide, the aspiring comedian, referred to it as the "Monument of Russo-Egyptian Misunderstanding."

This would have been the end of our exploration of Aswan, but our guide invited us to join a group he was taking to the Island of Philae. That trip was not covered in our program, but we gladly paid a bit extra for the adventure.

We were taken to the island in an overcrowded, sad-looking motorboat. I realize now that we were taking a considerable risk, but we didn't think of that at the time. It worked out well, in any case. The creation of the High Dam, and the ever-rising waters of the new Lake Nasser, had drowned the site of the temple dedicated to the goddess Isis and her son Horus. This and other temples had been dismantled after spending time under water, then rebuilt on higher ground; the effort was financed with the assistance of UNESCO. The temple opens on the *mammisi* (birth chamber), an antechamber, and the sanctuary itself. The reliefs on the walls must have been brilliantly colored before the flooding. These reliefs depict Ptolemaic kings and Roman emperors, disguised as Pharaohs, making offerings to Isis and her son.

We also saw temples dedicated to Hathor and Horus, and the ruins of a temple built by Caesar Augustus. Our excursion was crowned by a visit to the Kiosk of Trajan, also known as the "Emperor's Bed." A comparatively small structure with graceful columns and floral capitals, it was always considered something special. Located on higher ground, it had escaped the floods, and its original colors were still bright.

The next day was Palm Sunday. We were awakened early by the blare of the loudspeaker broadcasting religious services from the Coptic Church, on a hill across from our hotel. The Copts are Christians, descendants of the original inhabitants of Egypt. Their language derives from the ancient Egyptian language. The word "Copt" comes from the Arabic phrase "Qubt" derived from "Aegyptios," a name given by the Greeks to the people of Egypt. The Muslims shed this name, and it came to refer only to the Christian minority.

I wanted to go to the old city market to buy a walking stick, because all our trekking about was making my sciatic back pains act up. Ken went with me. On the way, I showed him some public drinking-water dispensers. These are no longer seen in the big cities of Egypt. They consist of large earthenware urns, chained around a tree. A tin can hangs on a string for the thirsty to dip into the urns.

We also saw some hole-in-the-wall shops, where we traded our dollars for some more Egyptian money, at a rate of over 50 percent more than we got from the bank. I found a serviceable solid bamboo shepherd's stick in the market. It was over seven feet long. I had it cut to size and bought it for a dollar.

Back at the hotel, Ken joined Steffi and Alice in the swimming pool. I went to the terrace of the bar, overlooking the Nile, to write some postcards and drink a cold bottle of beer.

In the afternoon we flew to Luxor, and checked in at the Winter

Palace Hotel. We were almost tricked into accepting a suite of two bedrooms with only one bathroom for both families; but I insisted that we should be given two separate rooms with independent bathrooms, which we got, plus a balcony for each from which we could watch the riverboats, owned by such international hotel companies as Hilton, Sheraton, etc., for tourist excursions, docked on the Nile right across the street.

Next morning I sat on the balcony, after getting up early to watch the street below come to life. The street sweepers were busy cleaning the walks, and a few horsedrawn carriages were parked along the road. I saw an Egyptian servant in his flowing *gallabiah* (robe) go around the riverboat, docked on the Nile across the street, beating on a gong to wake up the passengers. After breakfast we assembled in the hotel lobby with other tourists to wait for our guide. As I mentioned before, we were now in the ancient city which the Greeks called Thebes; its two districts are now called Luxor and Karnak. The ancient Egyptians called it Wast or Nu-Amon, which means City of Amon. On the western bank of the River Nile is the city of the dead; that is where the famous tombs are. On the eastern bank is the city of the living, where the principal temples dedicated to Amon-Ra, his wife Mut, and their son Khonon are located.

A ferry boat took us to the western shore and we were led to the Tomb of Tutankamen which was discovered almost intact in 1922, loaded with precious funerary equipment. These were moved to Cairo Museum, to be seen and appreciated by all visitors. What one sees now in the tomb are imitations of originals. The tomb escaped being looted by grave robbers because it was buried under the rubble from a tomb dug above it. We then visited the tomb of Ramses VI, with its elaborate drawings on the walls telling of all the good deeds the king had done in his life, to impress the gods in deciding the fate of his after-life. There were scenes from Egyptian mythology, reminding the viewer that even after death one has to overcome many obstacles such as snakes, evil spirits, etc., before reaching the final destination.

After a short rest and refreshments, we were led to the compound housing the temple of Deir el Bahari, built by the only female Pharaoh, Hatshepsut. The guide sat on a rock; he was a middle-aged, well-educated Egyptian, and his explanations were clear and simple. We stood around him as he spoke. He said, "In order to retain the name of the Queen remember that I am wearing a hat," and he pointed to his head cover; then he pointed to his suit, saying, "and this is a cheap suit; when you put them together, you get the name Hatshepsut." At this occasion, he gave a very enlightening lecture as to how the world had thought of Hieroglyphics as no more than decoration, until the discovery of the Rosetta Stone, which had three different sections with a different kind of writing on each, namely Hieroglyphics, Demonic, and Greek, all giving the same information. The Hieroglyphics were deciphered by Champlion, a French scholar who knew ancient Greek; this was an invaluable contribution to learning about the history of ancient Egyptian culture. The Rosetta Stone is now in the British Museum of London. Our guide also told us that, besides picture drawings and Hieroglyphics, the Egyptians had an alphabet of twenty-five signs which their scribes used every day, without realizing its worth. It was mostly used in business transactions and correspondence. It seems that the Phoenicians borrowed their alphabet from the Egyptians, and the Greeks from the Phoenicians; the Greeks passed it to the Romans, after making modifications, and we took our alphabet from the Latins. Our guide then showed us the colored carving on the walls, glorifying the naval expedition sent by the Queen to Africa in search of incense trees, the reception of the Queen's envoys with their gifts to the King of Punt (Somalia), and the returning ships laden with produce of Punt, including thirty-six incense trees, their roots protected by being in large baskets of earth.

In the afternoon we visited the colossal temples of Karnak and Laksur on the east bank, passing through the Avenue of the Sphinxes. We saw the Ptolemy Gateway, the temple of Khonsu, God of the moon, besides the temple of Amon-Ra and the different obelisks. We also saw scenes and inscriptions relating to the story of the divine birth of Amonhotap II, in which he claims (like

Queen Hatshepsut before him) to be the physical son of the God Amon-Ra. Centuries later, Alexander the Great made the same claim when he made extensive restorations to the temple.

Next day on our way to Cairo, we had a taste of a sandstorm when we had to wait in the plane at Laksur Airport over an hour. The sandstorm was raging outside with zero visibility. In Cairo, we were scheduled to go to a nightclub to watch some belly dancing. Instead, we decided to stay at the hotel and enjoy leisurely a good dinner.

On our last day in Egypt, we said farewell to Cairo and drove to the airport to catch a plane to Amman, Jordan. While we waited in line, some emancipated Egyptian came from behind and tried to get ahead of us. I mumbled loudly, in Arabic, words from an Arabic proverb, saying, "I wonder, is it by force or by turn!" Within a few minutes we heard the announcer on the p.a. system saying, "Please show respect to our guests and let them board the plane first." When we got to the plane, we were surprised to see the baggage neatly lined up a few feet from it. Each passenger had to place his luggage on a platform for loading onto the plane. I heard two versions as to why this is done; one is to make sure that the luggage is on the same plane as the passengers; the second is to avoid loading luggage containing a time bomb on the plane, as no passenger taking the same flight would do this.

Portuguese musicians in traditional costumes

German couple in traditional Bavarian costumes

Everywhere You Go, People Are the Same

Chapter 14,

Europe in the Spring of 1985

This year we decided to visit many countries in Europe. We went on our own, without hotel reservations. We always found good lodgings through travelers' help offices at the airport or railway stations.

We arrived by plane in Lisbon, Portugal on May 16, dead tired and went to sleep right away in our Hotel El Presidente. When we woke up we went by cab to the railway station to validate our Eurailpass. We found all the counters closed, so we decided to visit the "Alfama," the old city which is next to the railway station. We strolled through narrow, winding, picturesque streets until 6 P.M. when hunger assailed us. We found a typical Portuguese restaurant. It was very small with tables covered with white sheets of paper instead of tablecloths and uncomfortable wooden stools, but with friendly hosts. They immediately served us bread and "green" fresh wine and we ordered a native dish of meat and vegetables. We saw an impressive looking framed diploma displayed on the wall from the University of Peru, issued to the host, the Sympathetic Senhor Quintino Perreira for his great knowledge and experience in creating varied delicious dishes. We did not like his cooking and could not force ourselves to consume the blood sausage, nor the tripe, which were the main ingredients of the Portuguese stew.

The next day we visited the St. George Castle on a mountain, overlooking the Tagus river and the city. The ruins and the grounds of the castle are turned into a delightful park with moats and reflecting pools full of swans and other elegant birds. It seems that the beautiful park is really an attraction; it was filled with schoolchildren, tourists, and local people.

We took a leisurely walk down from the castle through the old city which was the only section of Lisbon that survived the great earthquake of 1755. It must have been a quarter of wealthy people, the houses were quite spacious and covered with ceramic tiles. They are now occupied by fishermen's families and poor people. Some of the tiles have fallen off and the houses look run down. Nevertheless, the neighborhood has lots of charm and beauty. On our way, we stopped at the cathedral and admired the old-fashioned, rickety, clanking street cars, climbing laboriously up the steep hill.

When we got to the railway station, we had a hard time finding the Eurail office in the maze of corridors. We validated our passes and reserved sleeping accommodations for our trip to France. We went back to the Alfama to a seafood restaurant. Steffi ordered a dish, "arroz marisco." She got a plate of mussels, and scallops, all in their shells that had to be removed by hand. However, the food was tasty, though messy. I ordered "bacaliau" stew, a tasty dish of codfish that I had eaten in Brazil.

After a rest in the hotel, we went for a walk along the Avenida de Liberdade, a short distance from the hotel. It led us to a square where a statue of the famous Marechal de Pombal was erected. Marechal de Pombal was in charge of rebuilding the city after the earthquake, and he did an excellent job. He created wide avenues, with greenery, mosaic sidewalks, and imposing buildings. Unfortunately, the buildings looked neglected and are run down. He also created a system of large parks in the middle of the city. We had ice cream in an outdoor café and bought a few souvenirs. On our was back to the hotel, we passed through some streets with buildings that must have been elegant. They had their walls defaced with graffiti, mostly about President Reagan's recent visit to Portugal, telling him to go home and take Prime Minister Soares with him.

Portugal is the poorest country in Europe and its people are mostly illiterate. The rate of unemployment is very high. A large number of Portuguese are away, working in Northern Europe. The people we met were very friendly and flattered, when we addressed them in their own language.

In the evening, we went to a nightclub with dinner and a performance of Portuguese folk songs, the famous *fadas* and delightful folk dances.

Next day we made a full-day tour in the vicinity of Lisbon by coach. We drove through very pleasant landscapes with fields, villages, small forests and undulating hills. The farms were small, mostly vineyards.

Our first stop was at Fatima. Fatimah was the daughter of the prophet Mohammed by his first wife Khadija. It is now a village and sanctuary in the Santarém district. The name must have survived from the time of the Moors (Muslim conquerors) when occupying Portugal. It is the site of an Apparition by Our Lady to three young peasant children on May 13, 1917. It attracts pilgrims from May to October ever year, and we were in Portugal during the month of May.

At first, a small chapel was built at the site of the Apparition. Later, the Church accepted the story of the children, and a huge basilica was built in an atrocious mixture of styles. The site of the miracle is now in a modern glass church, where a mass was celebrated during our visit. I pushed my way through the crowd of worshippers to get pictures of the original place.

From Fatima we drove to Nazaré (Nazaereth), a fisherman village. We stopped at the top of the cliff to enjoy a wonderful view and take pictures. We then proceeded to the restaurant at the beach for a meal of freshly caught fish and enjoyed the view of the Atlantic Ocean.

In the afternoon, we drove to a small town, completely surrounded by a city wall reminiscent of the Middle Ages. All the houses were freshly whitewashed and decorated with potted flowers, a real jewel.

Next morning, we went to the famous Gulbenkian Museum. Gulbenkian was an Armenian philanthropist who died in Lisbon on July 20, 1955. We were overwhelmed that one person could amass such a treasure trove of art. He left the bulk of his vast fortune, including the art collection, to a charitable foundation he had established.

The following inscription is in the lobby of the museum:

"I am fully conscious that the time has come to take a decision on the future of my works of art. I can say without exaggeration that I consider them as my "children" and that their welfare is one of my main preoccupations. They represent fifty or sixty years of my life throughout which I have brought them together, at times with innumerable difficulties, but always and exclusively guided by my personal taste. Naturally, like all collectors, I sought counsel, but I feel that they are mine, heart and soul."

—Lisbon, February 10, 1953
C. S. Gulbenkian

We were so carried away by our visit to this museum that we missed lunch in order to catch our bus for our afternoon tour.

The tour covered the National Palaces in Quelus and Sintra. The one in Quelus is a poor and small copy of the Palace of Versailles. Sintra is a genuine Portuguese summer palace in the mountains, decorated with all kinds of ceramic tiles, one room more interesting than the previous. It is surrounded by little gardens and gorgeous views outside the windows. After our tour of the palace, we saw a fiesta of folklore in the town square with young people attired in the different costumes of the county. Our return was along the sea coast, through the famous resorts of Cascais and Estoril, where many former heads of states have their fashionable villas. We took a stroll in the gardens of the famous casino, but did not go in to gamble.

On our last day in Portugal, we visited Belem (Bethlehem), a suburb of Lisbon. We passed near the famous Coach Museum, went through the Church of St. Jerome and saw the Monument of the Explorers. It is a masterpiece of ship in stone with sculptures of all the famous Portuguese explorers, beginning with Prince Henry and ending with Magallanes (Magellan), the first to undertake a voyage around the globe. We walked along the shores of the river Tagus to the Tower of Belem, oldest building of Lisbon in impressive Gothic style.

We arrived at the train station in time and the train left at 3 P.M. Our sleeping car was very old-fashioned and the seat was uncomfortable. The attendant advised us to sit in the dining car, which we did while enjoying beer and admiring the mountainous landscape between Portugal and Spain. Supper, as well as next morning's breakfast, was very frugal, probably adapted for what the majority of the passengers could afford. These were mostly guestworkers returning to their jobs in Northern Europe after a vacation at home.

We changed trains in Henday on the Bay of Biscay, the border with France. We were conveyed for a short distance to Bayonne, where we would change trains for Lourdes. Our train did not leave for several hours, so we left our luggage in the train-station lockers and went for a walk in the old city of Bayonne. Bayonne is in the Basque Region of France. The Chateau Vieux and the Cathedral of St. Marie built on the site of a Roman temple are worth visiting. The Musée Basque displays the distinctive features of Basque culture. Bayonne is on the famous coast of Biarritz, playground of the most famous people of the world. Incidentally, the only university in the Basque language is in Reno, Nevada, where there is a big concentration of people from Basque origin. We had ice cream in an open- air café near the river, and wrote lots of postcards, then went back to our train.

We reached Lourdes in the late afternoon. The tourist office was closed, so we went to the most inviting hotel from the several ones we saw from the train station. It offered an inexpensive room with bath.

Lourdes is a town at the foot of the Pyrénées, twelve miles southwest of Tarbes, France. In 1858, Bernadette Soubirou, a peasant girl, saw a beautiful Lady in a grotto who talked to her. The lady told Bernadette to come back to this place. Nobody believed her at first. But when the lady revealed herself as Mary of the Immaculate Conception, people came and watched while

Bernadette had her apparition and talked with the lady whom they could neither see nor hear. Finally, the lady told Bernadette to dig, and wash herself in the surging water. She obeyed, and her face became all muddy. Water came out of the spot where she had dug. A blind man washed his eyes in the water and recovered his eyesight. The Catholic church took over after authentication of the miracle by a commission of inquiry, appointed by the Bishop of Tarbes. A number of churches were built as well as a basilica. A schedule of activities was organized, i.e., masses, sermons, confessions, holy communions, way of the cross, candle-light processions and youth rallies. A quiet and solemn air of devotion is prevalent throughout the compound. Multilingual help is available, staffed by volunteers from all over the world, who wheel the sick around in little carts and on stretchers.

Actually, only a handful of unexplainable known healings took place in Lourdes, nevertheless faithful Catholics still flock to the shrine to bathe in the water, drink from it, and express their devotion.

Accompanied by Steffi, I stood in the place of the apparition, we drank from the water, and I lit a candle. In the evening we had a lovely French dinner near our hotel. The next day was completely spent in the beautifully landscaped park near the river, observing the pilgrims, visiting the churches, and following "the way of the cross" which goes up and down a steep hill, quite strenuous for Steffi. Larger-than-life-sized statues represented those who were involved in Jesus's walk to Golgatha.

In the evening, we participated in the candle-light procession during which the rosary is recited by loudspeaker. Each Ave Maria is sung in a different language. The real miracle of Lourdes are not the infrequent healings, but the satisfaction that the sick and troubled pilgrims get from the change of environment, the companionship with other sufferers, the tender care by the volunteer helpers and a renewal of their faith.

The following day we had a long train ride to Nice via Marseilles along the Mediterranean coast with views of mountains, beaches, the sea, and clean resort towns, separated by numerous tunnels. We were glad, when we finally reached Nice, in the French Riviera. The tourist office was already closed for the day and we did not like the looks of the hotels near the station. So, we walked, pushing our luggage, toward the town. We found a room in a respectable-looking hotel. We cleaned up and took a cab to the famous seaside Promenade. We ate in a first-class seafood restaurant. Steffi had, what she said, was the tenderest calamari she had ever eaten and I had a fancy cooked sole with almonds in a white-wine sauce. Of course, we had white wine to go with our food, and we enjoyed the nightfall effect at the water front. We watched the sun disappear in the sea, and the silent darkness of the night take over. We spent only that one night in Nice but went on to Monte Carlo where we checked in our luggage and went sight-seeing. We climbed to the palace, watched the colorful guards, the spectacular view of the Mediterranean, the harbor with the luxury yachts of the millionaires, and took pictures. We then bought postcards and stamps on our way to the casino. Steffi went to the casino to try her luck. I did not like the look of the casino which resembled a mausoleum; instead, I sat in an outdoor café and wrote a stack of postcards. Steffi was disappointed when she came back.

In Monaco were two different mail boxes to accept the outgoing mail. One is serviced by the local government, and the other by the French authorities. We sent our postcards through the local postal service, which had to be franchised with Monte Carlo's postal stamps and bear its cancellation. We went back to the center of town to consume a satisfying Italian lunch with wine. We picked up our luggage and boarded a train to Genoa, Italy.

We arrived in Genoa late at night and found a nice hotel near the train station. We had delightful authentic ice cream, and went early to bed.

The next morning we started our sight-seeing with a visit to the cemetery. On our voyage to Brazil in 1951, we missed a visit to the cemetery, while our fellow travelers raved about the beauty of this cemetery as the greatest tourist attraction in Genoa. We, however, were not impressed; the marble statues and crucifixes were loaded with a thick layer of dust, and soot and looked neglected. On the other hand, we enjoyed the splendid view of the town from the cemetery location. On our way back, we took a streetcar to Lido. We got to the beach after a seemingly endless ride through uninteresting streets and found a seaside park where children played under the watchful eyes of their parents. Back at the hotel a good dinner cheered us up. We took a window-shopping stroll before going to bed.

We took an early train next morning to Pisa. There we met a group of friendly young girls who went out of their way to help us. They showed us where to check in our luggage and put us on the bus to the cathedral. The church, baptistry and the leaning tower are in a large meadow, surrounded by the old city walls. It was the Sunday before Pentecost. Girls in white dresses, and boys in their finery were posing for pictures taken by their proud parents. The baptistry is separated from the main church, because, according to tradition, children are not welcome inside the church before they are baptized. That is why newly born children are first baptized, and afterward brought into the church. Most churches do not have a separate baptistry building, instead, they have a font at the entrance to the church.

Needless to say that the whole area was overcrowded with pilgrims, tourists and local people. Colorful booths lined the street where souvenirs and curios of all kinds as well as candy for the celebrating children were sold. Everybody seemed to enjoy the blue sky and the warm spring sunshine. It was an appropriate setting for the beauty of the cathedral, the baptistry, and the funny-looking leaning tower, which are all built of white and black marble. We found an excellent self-service restaurant outside the city wall near the cathedral where we ate an Italian lunch in a pleasant garden. The bus ride back to the train station passed next to majestic buildings, and through large squares. It was like a sight-seeing tour of its own.

When we arrived on the afternoon train in Florence, a long line had formed in front of the tourist office. An agent of a hotel convinced us to take a van to the Hotel Coralla, which was a clean, inexpensive place with a friendly and helpful host. He told us that on the next day, a Monday, the museums would be closed and instead booked for us a tour to Siena.

From the hotel, we went to the center of the town. Florence is one of the foremost art centers of Italy, second only to Rome. The Santa Maria del Fiore Cathedral is called the Dome, for short. In front of the Cathedral, a quiet crowd was waiting patiently for the arrival of their newly appointed Cardinal from Rome. Applause and jubilation accompanied his final arrival. He left his car, and followed a chanting procession into the sanctuary. We did not follow them into the crowded dome, but went to an outdoor café to watch a multicolored lot of people go by. Ladies in the most elegant and fancy finery alternated with elderly women in drab clothes, and carelessly dressed tourists. Men in blue jeans were followed by men in formal attire; a cosmopolitical mixture of people walked by in an endless stream.

The trip to Siena was very rewarding. We could not have wished for a more agreeable weather. We moved out of Florence into the lovely landscape of Tuscany. The rolling hills were dotted with vineyards, vegetable gardens, olive trees and greenery as we proceeded to the medieval town of Gimignamo, the City of the Beautiful Towers. We left the bus in a park outside the city walls and entered the city on foot. We were told by the guide to be back in two hours and try the famous wine of the city. A narrow street led us to an open piazza, surrounded by ancient buildings. On the way to the Gothic cathedral, I snapped a picture of festively dressed carabinieri (peace officers), walking outside the church. We then had a taste of the recommended wine, which we did not like.

The bus ride to Siena was short and pleasant. Again, we had to leave the bus outside the city and proceeded on foot to the center of town. After lunch we met our local guide who led us on a walking tour through the city. She was a very erudite and witty elderly lady who imparted the lore of her interesting home town with information and anecdotes. We went into courtyards and churches, saw the beautiful dome, the baptistry, and visited the museum. We gained an overwhelming wealth of knowledge about the first Christian families of bankers in Europe, native sons of Siena. After a last look at the harmonic town square, scene of the famous yearly horse races, we boarded the bus back to Florence.

The next day was devoted to Florence. We booked a tour for the afternoon to see the Ufficien Museum and other places of interest. Then we did our laundry and bought an additional suitcase for all the souvenirs we had bought on our way. On our return to the hotel, we got a message that the Ufficien Museum would be closed during the afternoon. We cancelled our tour and rushed to the famous museum. We had just enough time to admire the great collection of Renaissance paintings before closing time.

Our next goal was the famous Ponte Vecchio (Vicchio), the bridge over the Arno River, with tiny jewelry shops lining both sides of the bridge, displaying glittering gold and precious stones.

We visited the dome and the baptistry in the afternoon, and after a long and tiresome walk, we reached the Church of Santa Croce (the Holy Cross) where many of the most famous Italians such as Galileo, Dante, Michelangelo, Leonardo da Vinci, and Machiavelli are buried.

When we returned to the Piazza Signoria, we found out the reason why the museum was closed: It was that they were filming a movie in front of the Signoria, the Ufficien Museum, and the Gallery of Fine Arts. The whole piazza was closed, but we could sit in an outdoor café and watch the filming.

We left Florence the next morning to visit Venice, in an overcrowded train. At first, we had to stand, but later, we found seats. In Venice again we were taken to a hotel by its agent. It was not fancy, but adequate, though rather expensive. Across the street was an attractive restaurant where we sat in a loggia, bordering the Canal Grande with its gondolas and boats. After the perfect meal, we needed a siesta. When we finally woke up, we took a roundabout ride on the canal which ended on St. Mark's Square. We walked through narrow streets along narrow canals with elegant shops on the street level, decaying upper floors and a bad smell from the water.

Next day we started with a motorboat sight-seeing tour which stopped at the Basilica of Santa Maria della Salute, which is on an island, and continued to a glassblower's workshop, where a worker made a beautiful horse, standing on its hindlegs from a fiery ball of molten glass, within a few minutes. The tour ended with a walk through the ghetto, where the streets are even narrower and darker and the houses are higher than elsewhere, because more and more Jews kept coming to live in the confines of the ghetto.

After the tour, we sat in a café on St. Mark's Square. We listened to live music, while watching the people and the pigeons. We spent a long time in St. Mark's Church, in the palace of the Doges, and walked across the Bridge of Sighs where the prisoners waited for their trial and/or their execution. These are the infamous cells with lead roofs, where the prisoners went crazy from heat and thirst. They were described by Casanova who achieved his spectacular escape on October 13, 1756 from there, in his famous essay "Histoire de ma Fuite" (Story of My Escape).

Our visit of Venice ended with a whole-day train ride to Munich, Germany. Our fellow passengers were an especially nice couple, both teachers from Bremen with their well-behaved eight-year-old son. The scenery through the Alps, across the Brenner Pass, was very lovely.

In Munich, the Europäischer Hof Hotel, where we were the year before, was full. We found a good room at the Hotel Monachia nearby. We washed up and went to the Augustiner Bräu where we spent a lovely evening with umpahpah music and lots of beer.

Oberammergau is a lovely village, 42 miles south of Munich, famous for the performance of its Passion Play. To express their gratitude at the end of the 1633 plague that struck the village, the villagers vowed to perform the Passion of Christ every ten years. On our first morning in Munich, we decided to take the train to Oberammergau. There were no performances that year, but we took a tour of the theater which was quite interesting. We then had a wonderful meal, and even visited a German flea market. In the afternoon, we took the bus to Schloss Linderhof, one of the many palaces that the crazy King Ludwig the Second of Bavaria has built. The palace is gorgeous, and the landscaping and park are delightful; but the most spectacular building is the artificial cave, where an open stage is constructed next to an artificial lake, where Ludwig listened in solitude to his beloved operas of Richard Wagner.

By the time our visit ended, the last bus to the train station had already left. We hitchhiked a ride with a nice elderly couple and got back to Munich in time for another dinner in the beer garden.

Next day was the most rewarding of our trip. We took the train to Berchtesgaden, a resort area, 90 miles from Munich and 12 miles from Salzburg, Austria. The castle that used to be a summer home of the Kings of Bavaria is now a museum. Above the town was the chalet of Hitler (The Eagle's Nest). From Berchtesgaden we took a bus to Koenigsee, the most beautiful of all the lakes in the Bavarian Alps. The sparkling clean water is a deep green, and the mountains rise vertically into the sky. We stayed on a tiny peninsula with a lovely small church and an exquisite restaurant, where we ate the best and freshest trout we had ever eaten. Great pain is taken to save the lake from pollution. Only battery-powered boats are allowed and only one family has the license to fish.

After the boatride, we walked in the village, but it began to rain and we had to take the train without seeing the famous salt mines. We met a nice, elderly English lady on the train to Berchtesgaden; she spent the whole day with us, and we enjoyed her.

We spent the next morning shopping, each on his own, and met for lunch in an open-air restaurant. In the afternoon, we went sight-seeing in Munich to places where we had never been before, around the residence of the former kings, along wide avenues where the museums and fancy shops are located. We celebrated farewell from Munich with an excellent Bavarian dinner; the restaurant was a little fancier than a beer hall, and the music was not so loud. After dinner, we went to a movie and saw the excellent Mozart film (*Amadeus*) dubbed in German.

After the movie we took the train to Berlin, where we had reservations in the sleeping car. The train was run by East Germany. It was not exactly high class, but somewhat better than the one in Portugal. It passed for a while through East German territory and the authorities checked our travel documents.

We got a nice, inexpensive room in Berlin in a pension near the Kurfuerstendamm (main street). It must have been an older home with large rooms. In the middle of the front part of the apartment was the "Berliner Stube" (drawing or best room) with a door to the entrance vestibule and doors to the living rooms as well as a door to the back part of the flat, where the bedrooms, kitchen and bath were situated. Our high-ceilinged large room was in the front part and had French windows, leading to a small balcony where we could hang our laundry.

We spent the morning sight-seeing near the Kurfuerstendamm, shopping and exploring the ruins of the Gedaechtniskirche (Kaiser Wilhelm Memorial Church) that has been left standing after the bombing as a ruin, and the new, modern Memorial Church that was built next to it. In the afternoon, we took a guided tour through West Berlin that had changed so much that Steffi could not have found her way around any more. We saw what has been built new, and what has survived the ravages of war. We stood in silence in front of the infamous wall. We visited the rebuilt Reichstag (German Parliament) and had dinner in one of the many restaurant on the Kurfuerstendamm.

We had planned to go together to East Berlin, the next morning, but Steffi suffered from hay fever and could not go. I took the camera and went by myself. I stood in line to be processed at "Checkpoint Charlie." I gave them my passport with $30. They refunded me the $20 visa fee and said that Americans don't need to pay for the visa and gave me East German marks for the $10, which is the minimum that every visitor to East Germany had to spend there. People were very friendly in East Berlin. I had to ask some officers for information. They saluted and gave me the information very politely, and addressed me as "Sir." My first visit was the German State Opera House on "Unter den Linden," and the Hedwigs Kirche, then the Brandenburg Gate, and on my way, I had a chat with workers, working on the renewal of the Huguenot Church, of the Protestants that were chased out of France in the 16th century after the infamous massacre of St. Bartholomeu. I went back to West Berlin after visiting the German Emperors' Palace, passed by the University of Frederick the Great, and watched the goose-stepping changing of the guards. I would have like to see the Alexander Platz and the Soviet War Memorial in Treblow, built with red marble from Hitler's Chancellery, but there was no time.

I was just in time for the afternoon tour to Potsdam, East Germany, narrated by an East German guide who was well educated and very interesting. A lot has been done by the East German government to restore and preserve the historic buildings and gardens. We visited Sans Soucis, Frederick the Great's second palace and its wonderful park; we saw many historic and modern buildings and ended up in the place of the Potsdam Conference of the Allied Powers, which is now a museum with pictures of all the conferences during and after World War II in which the fate of the world was decided. At last we got a coffee break of good coffee and a rich cake in the Cecilien Palace.

On the trip back to West Germany, we had to go through a lengthy pass control to make sure that no East Germans were smuggled out. We arrived in time to get to the Theater of the West to watch a performance of the "Zigeuner Baron." It was a mediocre performance, and we were both tired and hungry. What do you think we ate? Hamburgers and French fries at the Burger King. It tasted like a million.

The train ride the next day to Hamburg took a long time, because of the border control by the East Germans. Hamburg, the "Gateway of the World," is the largest seaport on the continent of Europe. We took again a hotel near the railway station, inexpensive, and with a rich breakfast included. The breakfasts in all German hotels are a veritable feast of sausages, cheeses, butter, a variety of jams, honey, eggs on request, and coffee or tea. We spent the afternoon and evening walking to the Alster River and its lake. On our way back to the hotel, we saw ladies of the night in house entrances, movie houses, showing pornographic films, and the all-pervasive sex shops.

Next morning, we took a guided bus tour through Hamburg, which did not impress us very much. This was followed up by a pleasant boat ride through the large international harbor, and an even more pleasant gourmet lunch in a restaurant, overlooking the port. We had to rest in the afternoon to digest the opulent meal and drinks. In the evening, we saw a delightful variety show.

We boarded the wrong train from Hamburg to Frankfurt. It also went to Frankfurt, but on a longer route via Cologne through the lovely wine country of the Rhine Valley, which we enjoyed very much.

In Frankfurt, we called our son John's friend Keith from the hotel. He had a job with an American company in Bad Homburg. We arranged to meet him the next day. Keith, his wife June and young son, met us at the railway station and gave us the tour of Bad Homburg, a resort area with hot springs. Keith then drove us to Heidelberg, where we took the cog railway to the ruins of the castle that is so famous for its history and beauty. Back in town for lunch, a folk festival was in progress with performances of bands and dancers in colorful costumes from different regions. Many different foods and drinks were also for sale. It was hard to make a choice. Each one picked his favorite food and enjoyed it. Then we walked through the streets of old Heidelberg, the famous University town. We took refuge from a sudden rain in a typical German café, where they served us an excellent coffee with cake. Heidelberg was the last crowning highlight of our trip.

We were more than ready to return to our lovely Napa Valley, which we did the next day with a few hours' stop in New York airport, where we met Steffi's cousins Erika and Reni and had a nice get-together.

(Steffi deserves credit for her assistance in compiling this lengthy travelogue.)

Dikran, Jacob, and Kevork Orfali (from left to right)
at the Castel Gondolfo, Italy

Chapter 15.

Trip to Italy, Jordan, and France

In January 1987, my wife Stephanie and myself were invited to the Golden Wedding Anniversary of her brother Wolfgang in Jerusalem, Israel. I thought I better not travel in the cold winter on account of my arthritis. Instead, I built a Ming tree with fifty gold coins to commemorate the occasion, which Stephanie, accompanied by our granddaughter Veronica took with them to represent the American Orfali clan. On their way they stopped in London and took a side train trip to Scotland which they enjoyed very much.

Stephanie and I usually travel together. In order not to be shortchanged, I determined to visit Rome, Italy; Amman, Jordan and Paris, France where my brothers and sister are living. So I was able to reap praise for my just-published book *An Armenian from Jerusalem*, which I had sent to them a few months ahead. I left for Rome on my first leg of a 21-day excursion. My brother Dicran (Dick) with son Kevork (George) welcomed me to Rome on landing and drove me to Dick's house not far from the airport.

I have been many times in Rome before. This time I wanted to see as much as possible of the vicinity, so rich in historic sites. Accompanied by Dick, I visited the Vatican, the Coliseum, the Catacombs, watched the lazy Tiber River and other tourist attractions. I went to the Rome Jewish quarters and took pictures of the great synagogue that had made news recently when it was bombed by terrorists. I was watched by the Carabinieri (Italian police) on foot and in patrol cars who decided not to interfere.

Accompanied by my brother Dick, his son Kevork drove us to Castel Gondolfo, the summer residence of the Pope. We drove around the man-made lake, watched the fishermen, sailboats with multicoloured sails, took pictures. We had an exquisite Italian multicourse meal with the wine of the region, topped by local goat cheese, Italian gourmet sweet pastry, and cappucino coffee in a restaurant next to the Papal summer residence, overlooking the serene lake.

We also took a one-day trip to Naples and Pompeii. Pompeii was buried by the ashes of the volcano Vesuvius when it erupted in the year 79 A.D. It was accidentally discovered by architect Domenico Fontana in making an underground aqueduct at the site in 1594–1600. The excavation scenes of people in their chores of everyday life, suddenly stopped as in a movie—you could observe a pickpocket in the act of removing the wallet of a rich man, housewives kneading bread, couples making love, etc.

Another day we visited Tivoli, a town built on the terraces of the temple of Hercules Victor, and marveled at the different fountains at Villa d'Este, begun in 1549 by Pirro Ligorio for Cardinal Ippolito d'Este. We also admired the fine paintings of the Latter Middle Ages and early Renaissance in the cathedral.

From Rome, I flew to Amman, capital of the Hashemite Kingdom of Jordan. My brothers relocated their business and moved to Jordan from Jerusalem in 1948, before the partition of Palestine was implemented.

Amman

Amman is the site of the biblical Rabbath Ammon. Uriah, the Hittite who fell in the battle at the gate of Rabbath Ammon was placed in the forefront by order of King David, who coveted Uriah's wife Bathsheba, whom he later married. She bore him Solomon who succeeded him and built the Temple of Jerusalem.

In Hellenistic time, the city was renamed Philadelphia after its capture. It was one of the cities of Decapolis.

Amman regained its old name after the 7th Century. Many

remains of the Roman city, such as the Amphitheater, capable of seating 6,000, a ruined nymphaeum on the river, and remains of a temple on the citadel are tourist attractions. The Palestinians who flocked to Jordan to flee the partition wars and continuous hostilities contributed in transforming a sleepy, insignificant town into a modern city with magnificent stone buildings, first-class hotels, international restaurants and light industries. It is now enjoyed by Saudis and other Arabs with oil money who used to go to Beirut before the civil war in Lebanon.

Jerash

I visited Jerash, an hour's drive from Amman, with my youngest sister Nelly. The visitor can see an amphitheater, the ruins of Roman temples, a Byzantine church with well-preserved floor mosaics, a Hadrian Arch, and the remains of a crusader's fort.

Madaba

Madaba is another interesting town. An ancient map of the Middle East can be seen on the mosaic floor of the Greek Orthodox Church, which dates from the Byzantine period. This famous map was useful to many scholars in their research of the area.

A few miles from Madaba is Mount Nebo. Moses could see the Promised Land from the top of Mount Nebo. He was denied entry to the Promised Land by Jehovah for his lack of faith. Moses was irritated by the constant complaints of the Jewish people, he struck . . . the rock twice with a branch instead of just ordering it to give water as told by Yahweh. Water came out abundantly. The Lord said to Moses and Aaron, "Because you did not trust in me, to show my holiness before the eyes of the Israelites, therefore you shall not bring this assembly into the land I have given them." (Numbers 20: 9–12).

Petra

The ruined site of Petra, a rock basin on the Eastern side of the Wadi'Araba, was the capital of the Nabateans and a center of the caravan trade. Its entrance is through a narrow canyon between two high cliffs, which made it impregnable to an enemy, so that the city could be defended by a handful of soldiers. The Nabateans exacted toll and protection fees from the passing caravans to and from different adjoining countries like Egypt, Syria, Persia, and the Far East. The Nabateans lost their power when they got assimilated into the Roman culture and copied the Greek and Roman customs. Visitors to Petra marvel at the ruins of magnificent buildings cut into the rocks, the amphitheater, the cave dwellings with multicoloured natural rock formations in their ceilings and walls, surpassing any man-made paintings.

Nebi Musa (the Prophet Moses) is a small Bedouin village near Petra whose inhabitants supply and lead the horses used by the tourists visiting Petra. In the village, the traveler can see and drink crystal-clear cold water from "Ein Musa," the fountain of Moses. It allegedly was the result of a miracle when Moses struck the rock with his staff and water rushed out of it to quench the thirst of the Children of Israel during the "Exodus."

Agaba

The only sea outlet of the Hashemite Kingdom of the Jordan, at the head of the Gulf of Agaba or Aquaba. It may be the site of Glath, mentioned in the Bible, where the Romans had a military post called Aelana. From an old sleepy town built largely of mud brick, modestly used as a fort in World War I, the Jordanians have transformed it into a winter resort with many modern buildings with all the modern conveniences. They enlarged the port which is now able to handle many vessels.

Paris

My last stop was Paris, France. American visitors to France did not need a visa in the past. Things changed after frequent terrorist activities caused many French victims. Before leaving for my trip, I went to the French consulate in San Francisco to get a visa. In my application I mentioned that I would be visiting my brother who lives in France with his French wife and children. When I addressed the visa processing employee in French, he smiled and said, "I presume you visit your brother every year. You can have a multiple entry visa for three years if you wish. It costs a couple of dollars more, but will save you the inconvenience of applying for a visa every time you want to travel to France." I readily accepted and thanked him. Nowadays, U.S. citizens do not need a visa for France.

My brother Joseph welcomed me to France at Orly Airport. He drove me to Sevres, a Paris suburb, famous for its "China" works, on the way to Versailles, home of the French kings.

I wanted to spend most of the time with Joseph and family, and reminisce of old nostalgic events of our childhood. I was fully rewarded.

In short visits to Paris we took an excursion in a "Bateau Mouche," a fly boat on the river Seine through the city, visited the Sainte Chapelle (a church with exquisite stained glass windows, where the French kings attended religious services), the Notre Dame Cathedral, and went to the university, La Sorbonne, my brother's alma mater.

We ended up in the Latin Quarter, where we had lunch in a Tunisian restaurant, which from its name we thought it was Lebanese. The Latin Quarters, is Latin by name only. In it are represented all the United Nations. Restaurants and pastries bear foreign names and offer foreign cuisine. You can hear most of the world languages and very little French. We conversed in Arabic with the waiters , and were suddenly surrounded by all kinds of North Africans, some of them fierce looking. When we left my brother told me it is not advisable to visit the Latin Quarters at night.

We visited the St. Denis Basilica, resting place of the French royalty, to see the tomb of Leon VI de Lusinian, last king of the Armenians who was related to the French kings and died in exile in France. St. Denis brought back sentimental memories to my brother Joseph. He showed me the place of the barracks where the Germans kept him as prisoner of war during World War II. It was demolished, and turned into a parking lot.

We went for long walks, hiked in the woods around Sevres. We visited the site of the castle of St. Cloud, built on a hill overlooking on the river Seine, and the Bois de Boulogne. The castle was acquired in 1658 by the duke of Orleans, who built the palace later occupied by Napoleon Bonaparte. It was at St. Cloud that Bonaparte executed the coup d'état of the 18th Brumaire (1799) and there celebrated his marriage with Marie-Louise. Seized by the Prussians in 1870, St. Cloud was sacked to its foundation. There is a lovely park now where the palace stood.

We also looked at old pictures and enjoyed a leisurely family life. With our meals we tasted a variety of French wines and enjoyed the after-meal mandatory cheeses. I liked goat cheeses best.

My trip was crowned with a drive to Fontainebleau, the summer palace of the French kings, where they hunted in the vast forests around the palace. It is a town of northern France, 37 miles southeast of Paris. My brother Joseph accompanied by his oldest daughter Yvonne drove us there. It is a summer resort and the president of the republic frequently resides in the palace, one of the largest of the royal residences of France. Francis I caused most of the Cour Orale to be erected. Henry IV, Louis XIII, Napoleon I, Louis XVIII, Louis Philipe, and Napoleon III did their share of improvements and contributed to the splendor of furnishing it with priceless paintings and objets d'Arts.

Everywhere You Go, People Are the Same

Chapter 16.
Summer of 1988

꓿y wife Steffi wanted to attend a 50-year reunion of refugees from Nuernberg and Fuerth, at Stevensville in the Catskill Mountains in New York. We decided to meet in Boston after the reunion and visit New England and Canada.

In Boston we took a sight-seeing trolley bus, its very entertaining driver called himself Paul Revere. We drank duty-free tea at the Boston Tea Party reconstructed ship and crawled all over it. We also enjoyed the many little shops and street entertainers in the Fauneil Hall area.

We visited the Armenian library and museum in Watertown, Massachusetts. I saw my book, *An Armenian from Jerusalem*, on display. After lunch with the custodians of the museum, we browsed in the largest Armenian bookstore in Cambridge, Massachusetts, where my book is also available. We admired a beautiful view of Boston and the M.I.T. campus from across the Charles river, then found a way to the famous Harvard University. We walked through the campus, adjoining streets, and the quad. It looked much cleaner than the University of California, at Berkeley, and the students were better dressed.

A drive on scenic highways through lush greenery in New Hampshire and Vermont brought us near Northfield. Our friends the McKains live there on their Christmas-tree farm on a lovely hillside. Their home is a very old farmhouse, which is on the cover of their telephone book. We drove with the McKains through covered bridges and over a floating bridge to Montpelier,

Vermont, a tiny, sleepy town, and then went on to the Trapp Family Lodge. From here on our schedule had to be very flexible because of frequent rain.

At Burlington we ferried across Lake Champlain to New York State. We visited Ausable Chasm, which is a very narrow, steep canyon with interesting rock formations. One walks up and down and across bridges, sometimes near the water, sometimes high above. It was exhausting, but worthwhile.

In a Montreal suburb we had a lovely time with friends and their fat dachshund. We saw the Montreal metro and the beautiful Cathedral of Notre Dame. We found Quebec picturesque and intriguing. Ste. Anne de Beaupre is a Catholic shrine dedicated to Jesus's grandmother, a huge basilica where we saw the miraculous statue, crypt, and grounds. We passed an impressive huge waterfall. Back in Quebec we took the funicular to the boardwalk, admiring the gorgeous view, the palatial Chateau Frontenac and the street performers. In the old city, near the church of Notre Dame des Victoires, we strolled through the old narrow streets.

On returning to the New England states, we had whole lobsters in Maine, a messy but very tasty treat. On to Bar Harbor and Desert Mountain Island from Bangor, we found these to be real tourist traps. We had a clear and wonderful view at Acadia National Park from the summit of Cadillac Mountain. From the boat on the southern tip of Desert Mountain Island, we watched oodles of harbor seals on the rocks. A lobsterman brought up his lobster pot, which contained three lobsters and a crab. He showed us how to measure a lobster; small lobsters and the largest ones must be returned to the water. We handled the lobsters and crabs, after the lobsterman secured their pincers.

In Salem, Massachusetts, we visited the shop of the present-day Salem witch and the witches' museum, and proceeded to Walton. I wanted to drive to Providence, Rhode Island, and try to find the house of my first great love, an American girl to whom I showed Jerusalem in the mid-1930s. Claire had since died, but I continued to correspond with her mother. Anyway, we found the place where the house once stood. It had since been torn down and there was nothing much to see in Providence for me.

At Boston again, we spent a lovely evening near Fauneil Hall and the market hall, with the outdoor shops and street entertainers. We had Boston beans for supper, but were not impressed. The beans Steffi cooks are a lot better.

After our very restful flight home, our son Sebastian met us at San Francisco Airport.

Joseph Orfali at the tomb of Leon Lussinian, the last Armenian King

Chapter 17.

1989: Piestany Spa Cure Resort

My brother Leon and sister Nelly who live in Amman, Jordan, visited us four years ago. On their way, they stayed at Karlovy Vary (Karlsbad), "The Pearl among Czechoslovak Spas." The basic spa treatment consists of drinking naturally cold carbonated water, heat therapy with mud packs and compresses and tub baths, electrotherapy, diet, and physical therapy through reflex massage and remedial exercise. Czechoslovakia has been famous through the ages for its spas. My brother and sister brought brochures detailing the specialties of each.

I suffer from severe neck and shoulder arthritis, and sciatica in my lower back. I was treated by specialists in Illinois, the University of California Hospital in San Francisco, and specialists in Napa. The medicine they prescribed gave me temporary relief from pain, but the only thing that helps is physical therapy which I practice religiously every day. Our backyard spa also contributes its share of relief.

Out of curiosity, I wrote to the Czechoslovak Spa agency last year and received information. This year we were on the verge of booking a European trip to include Prague (Czechoslovakia) and Budapest (Hungary), when we received new brochures about the Czechoslovak Spas with prices we could not resist. We chose Piestany Spa Cure Resort for arthritis sufferers.

Having used our accumulated frequent-flier mileage to upgrade our tickets, we flew from San Francisco to New York as pampered first-class passengers. At J.F.K. the Czechoslovak Air-

Jacob Orfali   157

lines departure gate was next to the Pan Am gates. It looked like an oriental market or bazaar with complete chaos reigning; everybody jostled everybody else without consideration, children of all ages chased each other, dirty diapers were left in ashtrays, the noise was so loud that you could not hear your neighbor talking, and the toilets were dirty with water spilled all over and slippery. The worst part of it was that our plane took off 90 minutes late with the passengers milling around expressing their disappointment loudly.

When we finally went aboard we could not believe the multitude of people the plane could carry. Having flown first class to New York we felt that the seats were too narrow, but the flight attendants went out of their way to please us. They served free alcoholic and soft drinks, coffee or tea before, during and after the meals, which were fairly satisfactory. Most of the passengers were elderly people from different parts of the U.S.A. going to the spas or back to their country of origin to visit relatives.

Airports in Czechoslovakia are under military control. After waiting two hours, we went through screening of passports, visas and hand luggage and answered questions from military personnel. From a one-hour flight to Piestany via small plane, we went to Balnea-Esplanade, our hotel.

During registration we mentioned that my wife Stephanie needed urgent medical treatment because she had accidentally burned her breast with hot gravy while cooking before we left. She was treated at the emergency center at the time and was told to see a doctor upon arrival in Czechoslovakia. Here, the doctor who examined her recognized our name, saying that she had a patient by that name, but he came from Jordan. I told her that he was my brother. Then the doctor explained to my wife, "We will have to send you to the hospital in an ambulance. My nurse will go with you. We do not have the facilities nor the experience to treat you here. In the meantime you cannot undergo 'water treatments' until your burns heal." In five days, after three hospital visits, Steffi was able to participate in all the water and mud treatments.

They treated her right away without asking whether she had insurance or money to pay for it. On the contrary, they did not charge us extra, but considered it as normal medical expense covered by the fee charged for our stay in the spa.

We had a thorough treatment at the spa, based on the recommendation of the doctor who examined us, and time assignments by the central control. All appointments were punctual to the minute, and efficiently administered by a very helpful, courteous staff who spoke to each patient in their own language. The patients were mostly elderly retired persons from all over the world—Germans from East and West Germany, Americans, French, Greeks, native Czechs and Slovaks and other Europeans. There was also a large number of Kuwaitis with their own doctor in residence at the Spa who spoke the local language. Most Kuwaitis wore their national attire; men with long white robes, and some of the women were veiled, whereas the younger ones wore modern dresses. They lavishly spent their oil dollars buying everything in the shops. The Kuwaiti government contributed largely to the building and equipment of the spas and hotels, and there are quite a few of them in Piestany besides Balnea Palace and Balnea Esplanade.

There were a number of restaurants in every hotel. Guests were assigned a table and served promptly as they came in. Guests picked their choices from a list of menus two days ahead. Coffee and tea were free, but there was a low extra charge for beer, wine and soft drinks. Guests were asked not to tip the helpers to avoid conflict of interest. There were cafés with live music in every hotel and also singing cabarets. Many times we visited a bar that had live Hungarian Gypsy music where we had interesting conversations with guests from East and West Germany.

Along the River Va, full of swans and ducks with their young, we had several nice walks. We went to town, a short distance from the hotel, for window shopping. The shops were well supplied with everything; they even had a shop for imported luxuries for which one had to pay in hard currency, no questions asked. This explains why foreigners were accosted by well-dressed older ladies offering to exchange foreign currency for four times the official rate.

Briefly touring Bratislava, capital of Slovakia, we visited the palace grounds where the Empress Maria Theresa of the Austro-Hungarian Empire was crowned. We saw the theater building and University, the shopping center in the neglected old town and the imposing new bridge over the Danube which leads to Austria. Next to the bridge is a huge arc surrounded by new apartment buildings. It resembles a crane hauling containers from the ships on the Danube and dropping them inland. With us on the bus were some Kuwaitis who took the ride just to do some shopping, carrying large bundles on the way back.

One Sunday we took a day trip to the mountains. We were conveyed by ski lift to the summit where it started thundering and raining and was too cold for us to wander out of the café. We downed some stiff brandy and took the ski lift in the rain back to the valley where the sun was shining. On the last Sunday we attended a folkloric festival with local costumes, dances and music.

A well-educated Kuwaiti who was informed about world politics was assigned a seat at our table in the restaurant. He declared: "We are well aware of the tricks that America is playing in the world. It created Israel as a threat to the Arab Countries, it caused the Iraq-Iran war and supplied both sides with arms to bleed and weaken them, and it tried to involve Kuwait in the Gulf War by having Iran attack our ships. But we outsmarted President Reagan, a third-class Hollywood actor, who mesmerized the American public and laid claim to the leadership of the Western World. When the Russian navy started escorting our ships at our request, Reagan offered us a better deal, which was our aim to start with. We have our own invincible leader, Allah or God; he inspires his servants who direct our nation. That is why we don't have all the problems of drugs, unemployment, homeless and sick people without medical help, etc. God has given us enough petroleum revenue and it is shared with the poorest. Every Kuwaiti is covered by medical assistance from birth until he expires, and this also covers treatment in foreign countries such as this place. Kuwaitis pay a minimal fee for water, electricity and gas for their cars. Our hospitals have had air conditioning since the late 1940s. We have no unemployment; on the contrary, people come from all over the world to seek employment in Kuwait. We have the choice of maids from different countries to care for our children, also doctors and nurses for our hospitals. Our government pays for the education of our children even in foreign universities."

I asked: "Why are you so harsh with Israel? Are not the Jews your cousins, all children of Abraham, from Ishmael and Isaac?"

He replied: "Most modern Jews are descendants of the Khazars, a Turkish tribe who built a strong nation in Eastern Russia between the Black and Caspian Seas. They first accepted Islam, then had intermarriages with the Byzantine emperors, and finally found it convenient to convert to the Jewish faith for political reasons (independence from the Muslim Caliph and the Patriarch of Istanbul (Constantinople)).

"When the Khazar Empire fell apart between the 12th and 13th centuries, the converted Khazars migrated to Hungary and were welcomed in the newly acquired unpopulated land of Poland. These are the Ashkenasi Jews, descendants of Ashkenaz, grandson of Noah through Japhet, not Shem who is our ancestor and that of the Sephardic Jews. The politics of Israel are not that of a Semitic nation: they are rather that of godless Turks."

Our Kuwaiti friend should know that the State of Israel was created and internationally recognized by an irrevocable charter of the United Nations. Still, the excesses of the extremists should be stopped.

On June 12 I had a last dip in the mirror pool followed by a body massage, and after breakfast we flew to Prague. Customs formalities went smoothly, and we met some American school children returning from the Soviet Union at the airport who took our plane. We were pleasantly surprised by the roomy seats and gourmet meals and drinks, like first class. Time passed very quickly with all the pampering by the flight attendants. We reached New York ahead of time. A gate was assigned to us right away and we were at the customs area in a few minutes. Here a big disappointment awaited us; we had to wait ninety minutes for our luggage to be unloaded from the plane. Though we had hotel reservations in the J.F.K. airport area, we were subjected to an unfriendly reception and given a third-class room with minimum comfort.

Steffi's cousins Erika and Reni who live in New York came to welcome us back to the United States. When I went to get soft drinks and beer, I asked an elderly Black lady where I could buy what I needed. She told me that there was a shop right across the playground next to the hotel, adding: "Hurry up, Honey, don't stay after dark." One cannot imagine the terror New Yorkers are living through with no end in sight. Thank God we live in Napa.

Our first-class flight back to San Francisco was enjoyable. The United Airlines waiting rooms were orderly and the toilets spotlessly clean. We were again spoiled by the flight attendants who prepared each menu separately and kept offering us more and more free drinks, coffee and tea, etc. God bless America, especially our little nest in the lovely Napa Valley.

Our trip was quite a pleasant experience, we both feel that we have benefited from the different therapies. We also enjoyed visiting new places and meeting people of different cultures.

*Stephanie and Jacob Orfali at the celebration of their
Golden Wedding Anniversary*

Everywhere You Go, People Are the Same

Chapter 18.

Our Golden Wedding Anniversary, Napa, August 1989

We celebrated our Golden Wedding Anniversary on the last weekend of July, 1989.

Preparations began long before Christmas, 1988, when our children and grandchildren with their mates flocked into Napa for the family Christmas celebration. On this occasion our son George told me that all the chores were distributed and asked me for a list of guests to invite. Invitations were sent during January to enable people to arrange their schedules. George called everyone to confirm the invitations.

The first guest to arrive was my niece, Yvonne Orfali, on July 8. She teaches in a school near Paris. Putting her school vacation to good use, she practiced her English and prepared lessons about the U.S.A. with an emphasis on California and Texas. (She had spent a week in Houston.) We drove her to Lake Tahoe, Reno, Virginia City and the winter ski resorts in Nevada.

Our daughter Gabrielle with husband Frank and grandson Frank Anthony arrived on July 26, granddaughter Veronica came on the 27th, and George and Judy on the 28th. Our California children John and Sebastian with their mates helped accommodate their brothers and sisters.

Steffi's cousins Erika and Reni, whom we had met in New York on our way back from Czechoslovakia, were unable to come due to complications with health and grandchildren.

We had a banquet with many toasts at the Domaine Chandon champagne winery on the 29th, where, in addition to the company of our children with spouses and our granddaughter, we had the pleasure of getting acquainted with the Doyles of Kansas City, Missouri, parents of John's fiancée Mary.

The big celebration, attended by over sixty people, began at five o'clock on the 30th at our house, patio and garden, decorated with balloons, "happy anniversary" signs, golden streamers, etc. Gourmet foods were plentiful as well as soft drinks and beer. George made sure that the glasses of champagne drinkers were constantly replenished.

We had two anniversary cakes: a large one, provided by the children, and a small one, donated by Albertson's supermarket who were celebrating their own fiftieth anniversary in business.

We received many compliments from our friends who congratulated us for having such wonderful children and that they rarely had such a good time in their lives.

Our telephone line was busy conveying to us good wishes from the family in France, Jordan, Israel, besides the U.S.A.

Lots of love and devotion were contributed by each one of our children to make the unforgettable celebrations a real success.

Everything was done without outside help, with flawless cooperation and coordination in spite of the fact that our children live in different parts of the U.S.A.

What more blessings and sense of fulfillment can parents ask for? We are bursting from pride.

A Toast by Steffi on the Occasion of Our Golden Wedding Anniversary

Please fill your glasses for a toast
To people that we cherish most.
It is to our children four
And to their spouses, which is more.

Dear George is our firstborn son,
He lit our lives more than the sun.
He was so lovely and so slim
Though nowadays there's more of him.
He was quite clever from the start
And even now, he's very smart.
He chose as wife fair Judith Lee.
She's still as fair as you can see.
He travels to countries of every sort
It seems that never he gets bored.

Our only daughter, Gabrielle Marie
Was quiet and fat, but you can't see,
Because now she's slim and very clever
And troubles she did cause us never.
Her Scaccia husband Frank is such
That everybody loves him much.

Together they gave us our greatest joy,
Two lovely children, a girl and a boy.
Veronica married Stuart, a most handsome man
And works as a nurse, whenever she can.
Frank Anthony is a student now
But hopes as an actor to take many a bow.

Joe Sebastian was always very bright;
In school he was a shining light.
But when he grew up he liked women more—
I think he loved more of them than a score.
But now he is faithful, since he got her,
His only love is Beverly Potter.

John Paul is our youngest boy.
He was cuter than a Christmas toy.
In Brazil and in Zion he grew up neglected
Because both of us had to work as expected.
Nevertheless he was never a failure,
He became a computer expert and a sailor.
But his greatest accomplishment far and wide,
Is that he found Mary, his lovely bride.

So, drink to their happiness and health
Because they are our greatest wealth.

Jacob Orfali   167

*Stephanie and Jacob Orfali's Golden Wedding Anniversary
celebration at the Domaine Chandon, Napa County*

Chapter 19.
Our Spring Vacation 1990

Last year my wife Steffi wrote for a Jewish magazine about her great-grandfather David Ottensooser, a Jewish painter who lived in Baiersdorf, a little town in Mittelfranken, Bavaria. A year later, she received a letter from a Mr. Ralf Rossmeissl who worked for the county government of Mittelfranken which was creating a Jewish museum to be located in Fuerth, Bavaria. This museum would have exhibits about the history, customs and achievements of Jews in the county of Mittelfranken, where numerous Jews lived in Nuernberg and Fuerth and in small towns and villages. He asked for information about David Ottensooser to include an exhibit on him in the museum collections.

Steffi told him she would like to collect material and take it herself to her native city, Nuernberg. She had copies of a diary that David wrote from 1838 to 1842 while he studied painting in Munich and Dresden. Her cousin Renate Busse, another great-granddaughter of David Ottensooser, contributed a hand-painted plate from David's china factory, and her brother Werner Braun, a famous photographer in Israel, made a color picture of David's painting of his mother, Maiele.

Last year, my wife and I had visited Czechoslovakia where we spent most of our time in the health spa, Piestany. We welcomed going back to Europe and combining business with pleasure by visiting Vienna, Budapest and Prague after our meeting in Germany with Ralf.

On the way we saw our grandson, Frank Scaccia, graduate

Jacob Orfali   169

from Milliken College in Illinois, and spent a day with our daughter and son-in-law in Libertyville there.

On the flight to Frankfurt, there were a number of babies aboard who took turns expressing their aches and pains with crying. We had a sleepless night. In Nuernberg, we stayed at the Hotel Burghof, a cute little hotel in the Old City near the city walls and the historic castle. Steffi's brother Heinz and his wife Hadassah, who live in Israel, met us at the hotel. Heinz is president of my wife's family business, a cosmetics factory in Jerusalem. He had been in Holland with a group of Israeli businessmen for talks about trade between Israel and the Netherlands. We ate in the "Bratwurstgloeckle," a famous Nuernberg restaurant specializing in tiny fried sausages with sauerkraut and German-style roasted potatoes, together with plenty of Nuernberg draft beer.

The old city of Nuernberg was completely destroyed by the Allied air raids during World War II, but has been beautifully rebuilt in the medieval style for which the city, called the German treasure chest (das deutsche Schatzkaestlein) was famous.

We drove together to the Ludwigshoehe, a suburb where Steffi's family used to live when she was a child. Then we walked in the forest where the Braun children passed many happy hours, picking berries, mushrooms, and wildflowers. We also took pictures of their old, much changed house. We went through other small towns in the vicinity, all connected with their childhood memories. Steffi asked Heinz to go to the nearby sleepy village of Ottensoos which consisted of a church and a few shops. When Jews had to take family names during Napoleon's occupation of Bavaria, David's father who was born in Ottensoos, took the name of Ottensooser.

In the evening, Ralf Rossmeissl came to the hotel to take us out to a well-known "Weinstube" for dinner. Steffi's cousin Betty Gradmann from Jerusalem joined us, bringing the beautiful color photo of David Ottensooser's painting. We celebrated our family reunion.

Unlike in France or Italy where they serve you croissants, rolls, butter, jam, coffee and milk, breakfast in Germany and Austria is a big meal—a buffet of cold cuts, various cheeses, yogurt, cereals, eggs, juices, coffee, tea or chocolate, and an assortment of breads. Ralf joined us for breakfast while we planned our day.

The first stop was Fuerth, Nuernberg's sister city; while Nuernberg was a forbidden city for Jews during most of the Middle Ages, Fuerth had a sizable Jewish community throughout history and was a center of Jewish learning. Ralf showed us the future home of the museum, an old Jewish-owned house that the government had acquired.

At Baiersdorf, David grew up and had his china manufactory, and Steffi's grandmother was born. Steffi had a photo of the house, taken around 1920, when the family visited Baiersdorf. This was our only clue. We had no street name, nor a house number. We showed the photo to many passers-by, but nobody could recognize the house. Disappointed, we went to the old Jewish cemetery, where we found David's mother's tombstone. Many other family members are buried in this cemetery but all the inscriptions were in Hebrew. Ralf showed the photo to an old lady we met. She recognized the house and led us to it. An elderly lady who answered the doorbell confirmed that her family had bought it from David Ottensooser and installed a weaving workshop in place of the previous china factory. We took pictures of the house and Ralf promised to return to investigate further.

We stopped at a village where Heinz once worked on a farm. During the 1930s, even before Hitler came to power, young Jewish people realized that it was time to leave their homeland. Many emigrated to America, England and other countries, but it was difficult for people without capital to emigrate to "Erez Israel," the British Mandate of Palestine. Only a limited number who agreed to become farmers received immigration certificates distributed through the Jewish Agency. Heinz had just finished high school and decided to learn agriculture and to work as an eleve (volunteer) on the estate of a Jewish baron who was able to conceal his Jewish identity. Even Heinz did not know that his boss was a Jew, until we met a historian in the castle who told us about his background.

We drove through the Franconian Swiss, a very scenic part of Franconia where Steffi and her brothers had spent happy vacations during their childhood. We had lunch in a beer garden and visited a museum and an old synagogue in a picturesque mountain village.

That evening we were invited to an elegant restaurant by Steffi's second cousin Werner Rosenfelder, whom she had not seen since he was three years old, and his wife. Werner's father, Albert Rosenfelder, was Steffi's first cousin who married a Christian girl. During the Third Reich, Albert was able to get a tourist visa to the United States, where he worked as a stevedore on the waterfront of New York City until the end of World War II, when he was shipped back to Germany as an illegal alien. His wife Tini had remained in Germany with her three small sons and her mother. She raised the children as Christians and worked hard as a traveling saleswoman. Her house was bombed out, but her family survived. When Albert came back, he bought the Braun's furniture business because none of the Brauns wanted to return to Germany. Albert became a millionaire, and now his sons have inherited the thriving business.

That night Steffi had an attack of asthma and bronchitis and was awake all night long. We said good-bye to Heinz, Hadassah and Betty and took the train to Vienna. After Steffi had another very bad night, I went to the hotel manager. He said that it was impossible to find a doctor during the weekend. When I insisted, he suggested: "You can take a cab to the hospital of the 'Barmherzige Brueder' (Brothers Hospitallers). They refuse nobody." This Order of Charity for the Sick was founded by St. John of God, born in Montemor Novo, Portugal in 1495. He was a shepherd, then fought the Turks as a soldier in Austria. Influenced by the sermons of John of Avila, he determined to devote his life to the service of the poor.

We went to the hospital, where there was only one patient ahead of us. The doctor ordered an EKG and a blood test. He shortly received the results and prescribed medicine. Refusing to accept money for the treatment, he showed me a collection box and said, "Just drop what you feel like in that box." When he heard that I was an Armenian, he urged me to visit the Armenian Mekhitarist monastery whose abbot was his patient. The Mekhitarists are Armenian followers of St. Benedict.

Back in the hotel, I tucked Steffi into bed. She insisted that I should not stay in. I visited St. Steven's Cathedral and St. Peter's Franciscan Church where I took pictures of a statue of St. Sebastian for our son Sebastian. On Sunday I attended a High Mass at the Mekhitarists celebrated by the abbot with a substantial Armenian community attending. The assistant abbot welcomed me, offered me liqueur made by the monks and took me on a tour of the monastery's museum and extensive library. He spoke about the history of the founder and how they bought the building from the Emperor Franz Joseph of Austria. That afternoon, since Steffi was feeling a little better, we had a boatride on the Danube River.

Our cabin mate on the train to Budapest was a young man from Brazil. We had a very enlightening conversation in Portuguese about the present situation in that country. Having lived in the city of São Paulo from 1951 to 1957, we could still speak the language. We had a very good meal in the dining car, including goulash, Tokay wine and Hungarian specialties. At the frontier, the Hungarian authorities removed a Japanese girl from our cabin and the train because she did not have an entry visa in her passport.

The Hotel Volga in Budapest was very comfortable and compared with the best European hotels. Since Steffi's asthma and bronchitis had started acting up again, the hotel arranged for an appointment for us at the medical clinic. The doctor was waiting for us when we arrived. She was very helpful but could speak only Hungarian which we did not, so we succeeded in communicating through sign language, German and English. Steffi underwent tests, and antibiotics and cough syrup were prescribed. The doctor would not accept any money; by law everybody is insured in the socialist countries. When I insisted on paying, she accepted the equivalent of $5.00. At the pharmacy, I went to the window where the prescription was priced, I paid for it at a cashier window and finally went to the druggist who gave me the medicine. After Steffi got worse in the middle of the night, I cancelled our Prague reservations and our remaining two nights in Budapest.

We used our Eurail passes to travel through Munich to Fuessen in the Alps, hoping the clear air would improve Steffi's illness. Things did not get better at night. The doctor who examined Steffi gave her a shot to help her sleep and told her to see him the next morning. Being foreigners, we were not covered by the "Socialized Medicine" as all Germans are. The doctor presented us with a stiff bill, which we paid. Doctors in Germany are allowed to have private patients.

We took a bus to "Hohenschuangau" to see the fairy-tale castle "Neuschwanstein." From the bus stop, we went by horsedrawn carriage to a landing on the mountain top. While Steffi rested in an open-air restaurant, enjoying the scenery, I climbed the remaining distance to the castle. In spite of the large number of visitors to the area, the landscape is as unspoiled as at the time of the Bavarian "Mad King Ludwig II" whose hobby was building exquisite castles. Neuschwanstein is the jewel of the Bavarian castles he built. Its turrets and battlements inspired Disney's "Sleeping Beauty" castle. Nothing can blur the magic of the first sight of the turrets and crenelated battlements. I can still hear the clip-clop of the horses' hooves bearing us uphill. Inside the castle, the grand murals depicting scenes from the "Nibelungenlied," "Tannhauser," and "Parsifal" are awe-inspiring. The gilded walls and ceilings, opulent hand-embroidered draperies and wood carvings are stunning. The next day we joined a bus tour to the three countries, Germany, Austria and Switzerland which border the Bodensee (Lake Constance), and the "Flower Island of Mainau" in the Bodensee.

After flying home from Frankfurt, we were happy to be back in Napa. With several weeks' rest in the familiar ambience, Steffi is now well again.

About the Author

Jacob George Orfali (Hagop Khatcherian) was born of Armenian parents in Jerusalem in 1915 during the Ottoman rule. His roots and early life are described in Jacob's first book *An Armenian from Jerusalem*. He grew up amid the cultural diversity under the British Mandate of Palestine, and was educated at the Christian Brothers' college in the Holy City of Jerusalem. Jacob worked as a translator at the Jerusalem Police Headquarters under the British Administration during the 1930's and 1940's. During the 1940's he was traveling auditor for the Socony Vacuum Oil Company (Mobil Oil) in Jerusalem, Beirut and Damascus. Jacob reorganized the accounting classification system for the United Nations Headquarters at UNESCO in Beirut during the early 1950's. After moving with his family in 1951 to Sao Paulo, Brazil he was managing cost engineer for hydroelectric power projects with Sao Paulo Light and Power and member of the Brazilian Industrial Standards Association. Jacob and his family moved to the USA in 1957. At Abbott Laboratories in North Chicago, Jacob served as cost accountant during the late 1950's. During the 1960's and 1970's he managed a rural route for the U.S. postal Service in Zion, Illinois.

Jacob is fluent in nine languages, which he acquired through interaction with people from many cultures. He and his wife Stephanie now make their home in Napa, California. They have a loving relationship with their four children and three grandchildren. Jacob and Stephanie have traveled extensively in the Middle East, Latin America, Europe and the former Soviet Union as well as the USA, demonstrating how much living one can squeeze into a lifetime. Jacob Orfali's philosophy of life, demonstrated in his second book *Everywhere You Go, People are the Same* , is that people of diverse background and experience have the same aspirations and essential human nature.

www.ingramcontent.com/pod-product-compliance
Lightning Source LLC
LaVergne TN
LVHW051347080426
835509LV00020BA/3319